LOGOMOTIVE

RAILROAD GRAPHICS AND THE AMERICAN DREAM

LOGOMOTIVE

RAILROAD GRAPHICS AND THE AMERICAN DREAM

Ian Logan & Jonathan Glancey

Foreword by Norman Foster

SHELDRAKE PRESS
LONDON

First published in Great Britain in 2020 by
Sheldrake Press, P O Box 74852,
London, SW12 2DX.
Telephone: +44 (0)20 8675 1767
Email: enquiries@sheldrakepress.co.uk
Website: www.sheldrakepress.co.uk

ISBN 978 1 873329 50 4
British Library Cataloguing in Publication Data:
A catalogue record for this book is available from the British Library.

Frontispiece: Painted on the side of a diesel locomotive, the Missouri Pacific's eagle is a powerful symbol of dynamism and speed.

Endpapers: Ian Logan's photographs, taken in the 1970s, capture the number and variety of logos in use on the US railroads at the time.

Color origination by Eric Bailey Ladd at Pixywalls Ltd.

Printed in Singapore

EDITOR: SIMON RIGGE
Deputy Editor: Chris Schüler
Editorial Assistants: Phyllis Armstrong, Elena Silvestri Cecinelli, Francesca Hawkes, Bret Johnson, Beatrice McCartney, Sirli Manitski, Hannah Prutton
Art Direction: Bernard Higton
Picture Editor: Karin Robinson
Indexer: Elizabeth Wise

AUTHORS

Ian Logan was at the center of the design revolution that marked the end of post-war austerity. After studying at the Central School of Art and Design in London, he joined JRM Design, where he and his partners produced prints for fashion designers such as Mary Quant and Jeff Banks. His money boxes in the form of the classic red British telephone kiosk became known all over the world. Ian's passion for vintage railroad Americana was rooted in a childhood attuned to the sounds of folk, skiffle, and blues under the influence of his uncle, the folk singer Ewan MacColl.

Jonathan Glancey is a writer and broadcaster specializing in buildings, cars, planes, and trains. The architecture and design editor of *The Guardian* from 1997 to 2012, he now reports on those topics for the website BBC Culture and newspapers and magazines worldwide. His obsession with trains began in childhood, and eventually led him to drive an Indian Railways WP-class Pacific steam locomotive from Delhi to Chandigarh. It has inspired four books, *The Train: A Photographic History* (2004), *John Betjeman on Trains* (2006), *Tornado: 21st Century Steam* (2010), and *Giants of Steam* (2012), in addition to the Channel 4 series *Small Railway Journeys* (2006).

Norman Foster is an internationally renowned architect whose buildings include the Hearst Headquarters in New York, the Museum of Fine Arts, Boston, the Swiss Re "Gherkin" in London, and the Reichstag dome in Berlin. His passion for railways goes back to childhood, when he would watch trains passing his home in Manchester. He has undertaken several major railroad projects, including the Florence High Speed Station in Italy and four stations for the Haramain High Speed Rail in Saudi Arabia.

CONSULTANT

H. Roger Grant is a professor of history at Clemson University, South Carolina. Recognized as one of the world's leading authorities on American railroads, he is the author of more than thirty-five books, including *Railroads and the American People* (2012) and *The Louisville, Cincinnati & Charleston Railroad* (2014). Grant's latest book, *Transportation and the American People*, appeared in 2019.

CONTENTS

FOREWORD

by Norman Foster

In the 1940s as a pre-teenager I would stand for hours at the end of a *cul-de-sac* next to my home in a Manchester suburb waiting for a glimpse of an express locomotive, a "namer" in train spotter's language. The long waits were punctuated by the passing of goods trains, the leisurely rhythms of their steam locomotives, and by endless lines of wagons. If I stayed long enough, there would be the more urgent and higher-frequency sound of an express train that would suddenly explode into view. In a fraction of a second, the curved arc of the nameplate midway along the length of the boiler would flash by with its raised, polished fonts standing proud against a painted background, invariably a deep burgundy red or earthy green.

The sight and sounds of these machines belching steam and flying sparks with pistons, rods, and cranks whirring to a blur was a just reward for those uncomfortable and lonely waits. I ticked off the names in a *Locospotters* book published by Ian Allan, a pocket bible for enthusiasts like myself. This was also the era of *The Eagle*, a weekly publication launched in 1950 with beautifully drafted cutaway cross-section centerfolds bringing alive the then world of technology, including the latest trains.

With its on-board life of saloons and dining cars, the express train was always more than just a machine hurtling across the landscape. It conjured a romantic vision of adventure, travel, escapism, and high lifestyle. If this was true of the British Isles, then imagine the image of the railroad in faraway America with its diverse climates, vast distances, and endless horizons. Here, the express train, freight trains, and even entire systems were immortalized in hit songs. I remember "On the Atchison, Topeka, and the Santa Fe" sung by the Andrews Sisters, but it could have been Judy Garland or Bing Crosby with the Tommy Dorsey band. The US railroad was so embedded in popular culture that it constantly recurs in music over the decades. By the time I left Britain for America in 1961, Lonnie Donegan and his skiffle group's hit version of "Rock Island Line" was a familiar song.

At the same time, one of my later heroes, the photographer O. Winston Link, was finishing his documentation of the last days of steam in epic images of the Norfolk & Western Railway in rural Virginia. Link gave up a successful career with his own New York studio, and prestigious commercial clients, to pursue his passion.

The fusion of abstracted typography and graphic symbols permeates American culture and seamlessly transfers from the domain of engineering into the world of art. The stenciled white star and numerical data painted directly onto the khaki-colored body of the World War II Jeep, for example, resonate in works of the artist Robert Indiana.

The ultimate marriage of machinery, branding, graphics, color, and lifestyle found its apex in American railroad systems. *Logomotive* seeks to distil this rich and varied subject down to a single title word, yet turning the pages, it is an insightful overview, full of anecdotal diversions. It is a reminder of an American past when, to evoke the words of Gertrude Stein, "There was a there," and the railway systems magnified differences between places.

Logomotive touches on so many of my personal interests and the ways they connect, particularly streamlining, which ushered in the new era of lightweight, stainless steel, post-steam expresses like the Burlington *Zephyr* built by Budd of Philadelphia and Union Pacific's *M-10000*. Budd also pressed body panels for the revolutionary Chrysler Airflow automobile of the same period. In promotional photo shoots, the Airflow appears alongside the *M-10000*. Significantly, both are also visually linked to the Art Deco detailing of the New York Chrysler Building – all born in the early 1930s.

Ian Logan and Jonathan Glancey are to be congratulated for assembling such a rich collection of images with a strong narrative that captures the spirit of an age and its boundless confidence in creating a continental high-speed rail infrastructure. By inference, this is an object lesson for present generations of civic leaders and policy makers. China currently has 19,000 miles of high-speed track to America's 500 miles. The fastest journey from New York to Chicago takes nineteen hours. To cover the same distance in China takes four and a half. *Logomotive* is thought-provoking beyond the achievement of charting a great American graphic design tradition.

Norman Foster, Gilly, Switzerland, 2020

PREFACE

by Ian Logan

It was 1968, and a party was in full swing at Macy's. The New York department store was staging a Best of British design event, and had asked a whole crowd of us over for the opening. I was there with a number of other designers, including Habitat founder Terence Conran and Rodney Kinsman of OMK Design. Rodney and I were chatting to an American furniture importer friend, who asked,

"Are you doing anything this weekend?"

"No."

"Well then, you can borrow my Mustang."

This was an offer not to be missed, especially after the hell on earth that was the Chelsea Hotel, where nicotine was dripping off the curtains and the scuttling of cockroaches woke us in the

night. The adventure started next morning. Rodney and I went to a diner for breakfast and asked for ham and eggs times two.

"How d'ya like yer eggs, boys?"

"Er, rare?"

Young, naive, and inquisitive, we drove off into Bear Mountain, a state park north of New York, looking for an America we thought existed. We ended up in Cold Spring, then a run-down little industrial town. We were chatting to some local guys in a bar when the glasses started to rattle on the table and I heard a train approaching. I rushed outside and there, right next to the bar, was a railroad track. I couldn't believe what I was seeing: the train was emblazoned with the name Rock Island. My uncle was the singer and songwriter Ewan MacColl, and I was brought up listening to folk, skiffle, and blues, so of course

I knew Lonnie Donegan's recording of the "Rock Island Line," but I hadn't worked out that Rock Island was a real, operational railroad. The loco was pulling a long train of boxcars, one of which was painted with a big circle saying Seaboard with a heart in the middle and the slogan Through the Heart of the South. What a logo! I'd never seen anything like it, and I knew I had to explore this further.

I had drawing and railways in my blood. I went to art school at the age of twelve and spent the first four years of my working life as an apprentice draftsman at the Westinghouse Brake and Signal Company at Chippenham in south-west England, where the ruthless O. S. Nock, later one of the best-known railway historians of the 20th century, was Chief Draftsman. In those days, people who drew for work were called technical illustrators, industrial artists, or draftsmen. It was quite a humble calling. The term graphic designer was still unknown.

After art school and technical drawing, I went into fashion and tinware and was commissioned to design packaging for all kinds of products from tea and candy to talc and soap. Eye-catching graphics were my lifeblood. Excited by my encounter with the Rock Island Lines, I became very interested in the iconography of the railroads and started collecting books on American trains, but I soon realized that the focus of all those titles was nothing to do with the graphics – it was the lines, the locomotives, and their operation. I was fascinated by the imagery, and the names of the great passenger trains that were the inspiration for so many folk and blues songs: the *Orange Blossom Special, Midnight Special, Pan American, City of New Orleans*, and the *Wabash Cannon Ball* to mention but a few. Surprisingly, most of the logos, or heralds as they were called, were not the work of designers. They were created on the drawing boards of people working on the railroads in other capacities. They appear to have happened when someone in the

Page 10, above, and right: Inspired by the artwork I'd seen on the sides of boxcars, I designed eight signs based on railroad logos, had them made up in enameled tinware and posed beside a selection for a newspaper photographer when I offered them for sale through my studio.

Opposite: Johnny Cash perches on top of a Seaboard Air Line boxcar on the cover of his 1965 album Orange Blossom Special. The title track, inspired by the train of that name, was first recorded by Ervin and Gordon Rouse in 1939.

SEABOARD
AIR LINE
RAILROAD

THROUGH
THE HEART
OF THE
SOUTH

ROUTE OF THE
Silver Meteor

company said, "Look, we need a herald for the front of the train" and a draftsman in the engineering department or a ticket agent produced a sketch, or the task was put out to a public competition. They sprang straight from the operational railroad and its users, which is why they have such spirit and guts.

During the late Sixties and Seventies I made scores of journeys around the USA photographing as many freight cars, cabooses, and engines as I could find. The glory days of the US railroads were from the 1920s to the mid-1950s before air travel took over, and the passenger routes were very much in decline by the time I came along. Since then virtually all the logo-branded boxcars and cabooses have vanished too, and most of the private lines have been amalgamated into a very small number of huge companies, BNSF, Union Pacific, and CSX being the most prominent.

For me, the names of the great steam and diesel locomotives that hauled the passenger expresses still echo along the tracks: the Burlington *Zephyrs*, Rock Island *Rockets*, GM&O *Rebels*, Milwaukee Road *Hiawathas*, Louisville & Nashville *Dixie Flyers*, Wabash *Cannon*

Balls and, last but not least, the *Chieftains* and *El Capitans* of the Atchison, Topeka & Santa Fe Railway. This was marketing magic. There is a great advertising poster for the AT&SF from the 1940s when all the celebrities traveled by train. A beautiful film star is photographed by paparazzi on a station platform, with the caption, "She came in on the Super Chief."

Cataloging and recording the graphics and slogans created during those days of fierce commercial rivalry has been a love, a passion of mine for forty years. This book is my tribute to what must be the most exciting collection of graphic imagery ever to have been produced in this field anywhere in the world.

Ian Logan, London, 2020

In the distance hear her moanin'
Hear her lonesome whistle scream
It's the *California Zephyr*
The Union Pacific Queen

Hank Williams Sr.

One of the AT&SF posters that
I so love stars the glamorous
Super Chief all-room train with its
comfortable groups of armchairs
and an equally glamorous movie
star arriving in Los Angeles.

She came in
on the
Super Chief

How else would she travel to and from California?

For the Super Chief is one of the most glamorous all-room trains
in America, filled with people who know how to travel and
appreciate the best in travel.

It serves those famous Fred Harvey meals.

It operates on a 39¾-hour schedule between Chicago and Los Angeles.

The Super Chief is the flag-bearer of Santa Fe's fine fleet of
Chicago-California trains which run each day.

SANTA FE SYSTEM LINES ... Serving the West and Southwest

T. B. Gallaher, General Passenger Traffic Manager, Chicago 4

1. CONQUERING THE CONTINENT

Previous page: A Southern Pacific GP 30 locomotive hauls freight through desert in New Mexico. The SP logo is picked out in white against the company's "bloody nose" livery, which was used from 1958 to 1991.

Right: In John Gast's 1872 painting *American Progress*, three classic "American"-type locomotives follow the wagon trains of white settlers, bringing with them the infrastructure of the Industrial Revolution.

From the 1830s railways spread out from the East Coast of the United States, through what had been the founding colonies and on toward Chicago. The ultimate goal of railroaders, made manifest when the crazy days of the California Gold Rush started in 1849, was a transcontinental railroad connecting east and west coasts. Once achieved, this would forge a truly united USA and a national economy that for several generations to come would appear limitless in scope and ambition.

Without trains, it could take more than six months to sail from seaports on the East Coast to California via Cape Horn. Overland travel by wagon train was uncertain and often downright dangerous. The railroad, however, promised more than speed, convenience, and a safe passage across thousands of miles of wild frontiers. It spoke of the spirit of indefatigable progress as seen through the eyes of white settlers, evangelical politicians, real estate speculators, chancers, snake oil salesmen, and big-thinking entrepreneurs. And when the trains did cross America they also shaped a new aesthetic, that of a golden railway age combining engineering, art, advertising, architecture, poetry, music, and design.

If a picture could paint a thousand miles of railroad track in that pioneering, steam-driven era, *American Progress* is surely it. In 1872, George Crofutt, publisher of a series of popular transcontinental travel guides, commissioned John Gast, a Berlin-born Brooklyn painter, to illustrate what the majority of white Americans believed to be the enlightened and inevitable westward march of their civilization across the continent from the Atlantic to the Pacific.

Gast's painting depicts Columbia, a classical muse garbed in a diaphanous robe, flying serenely over the Wild West bearing a schoolbook in one hand and trailing a telegraph line from the other. Beneath her feet a succession of wagon trains, mail coaches, hunters, and white farmers oust bears, bison, and Native Americans seen fleeing westwards. Behind Columbia, three railroad trains steam along northern, Midwestern, and southern routes from industrious eastern seaports toward the Rocky Mountains and the promise of California.

Just three years before Crofutt commissioned *American Progress*, a ceremony had been held at Promontory Summit,

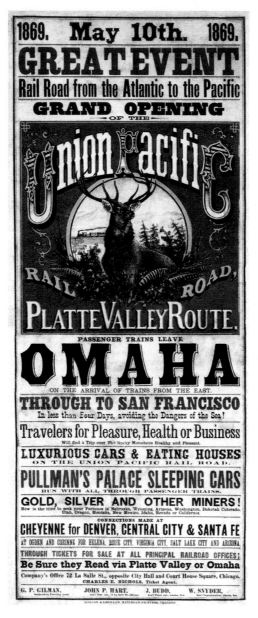

A poster advertising the opening of the Union Pacific Railroad in 1869 lures gold prospectors with a journey of less than four days from Omaha to California.

Utah, to celebrate the completion of the first transcontinental railway with the meeting of the Central Pacific coming from the west and the Union Pacific from the east. The photographer Andrew J. Russell was on hand to capture the moment. The defining image he recorded has been reproduced ever since. Samuel S. Montague, Central Pacific's Chief Engineer, is seen shaking hands with his counterpart Grenville M. Dodge of the Union Pacific, while engineers George Booth and Sam Bradford brandish the champagne bottles they broke over the smokeboxes of each other's locomotives.

The transcontinental railroad did indeed drive bears and buffalo away from newfound white settlements. It also played its part in reducing the numbers and destroying the way of life of Native Americans, supplying US soldiery with guns, ammunition, and telegraph warnings while boxing in Indian lands. To many, if not all Americans, the triumphant expansion of the railroads was one fulfillment of Manifest Destiny, a notion forged by John O'Sullivan, editor of the *Democratic Review.* In a drum-roll column written in December 1845, O'Sullivan spoke thunderously if controversially of "the right of our manifest destiny to overspread and to possess the whole of the continent which Providence has given us for the development of the great experiment of liberty and federated self-government entrusted to us."

It seems somehow significant that the herculean mixed freight trains that rumble and thunder across the great American plains and up and through mountain ranges are known as manifests. The word is derived from its early 18th-century meaning of a declaration, not as in independence or the rights of man, but in terms of cargo, of what a ship or wagon was carrying. Yet it is hard not to watch a mile-long Union Pacific freight train rolling across Wyoming or Utah today and not associate the railroad term, especially given the UP's advertising slogan Building America, with O'Sullivan's Manifest Destiny.

Enormous drive, energy, and sheer hard labor went into the completion of four commanding east-west railroad routes across the United States between 1869 and 1890: the Northern Pacific, Union Pacific, Atchison, Topeka & Santa Fe Railway, and Southern Pacific. These all radiated out from Chicago, the junction box of US railroads, with its established connections to New York and the Atlantic seaboard. South of Chicago, the Illinois Central – the Mainline of Mid-America – flanked the Mississippi on its way through the corn and cotton belts to Louisiana and New Orleans.

Entire railroads were surveyed, designed, constructed, and operated by officers seconded from the US Army Corps of Engineers backed by battalions of construction workers, many of them Irish immigrants, others, as in the case of the Northern Pacific, from Germany and Scandinavia, while great sections of the Central Pacific driving east to meet the Union Pacific were the work of Chinese laborers. Their skill and tenacity were something of a wonder of the early railway age, although, as they said, they were descended from men who built the Great Wall of China.

Their ultimate reward was the 1882 Chinese Exclusion Act signed by President Chester A. Arthur in deference to fears that Chinese laborers were undermining wages and taking jobs from all-American workers. So keen were unemployed white miners in Sweetwater County, Wyoming, to get rid of the Chinese, that on September 2nd, 1885 they robbed, shot, and stabbed them and, setting fire to their houses, burned them alive. No one was held responsible for the killings and no arrests were made. Some of those who managed to survive what became known as the Rock Springs Massacre did so by struggling aboard a passing Union Pacific train.

Most trains of the time were hauled by "American" steam locomotives, a name given by the *Railroad Gazette* in 1872 to a 4-4-0 type developed in the late 1830s and within a decade found hard at work across the continent. With their giant spark-arresting smokestacks, massive headlamps, prominent cowcatchers, and spacious cabs, these locomotives were soon considered as American as the Stars and Stripes and the Colt Peacemaker. They can be seen in John Gast's *American Progress*. Light on the track, easy to service, and with forgiving suspension, they were ideal machines for pioneering lines. More than 25,000 were built and they were still at work on backwater railways in the twilight of US steam in the mid-1950s.

The invention of highly effective air brakes by George Westinghouse in 1869 allowed trains to be longer and heavier and spelled the end of the American type on front-rank duties. From the 1870s US locomotives grew and grew. If they tended to share a common look, this was because few railroads designed and built their own engines. By World War I, most were constructed by the mighty triumvirate of Alco (New York), Baldwin (Pennsylvania), and Lima (Ohio).

Toward the end of the 19th century, railroads sought increasingly to establish corporate images very much their own. One reason was the Trademark Act of 1881 that protected symbols or logos, so encouraging companies to design readily identifiable graphics. From the completion of the transcontinental railway in 1869, railroads created what was in effect a single market for goods across the country. Products that had been the preserve of consumers in California or Connecticut were now available nationwide. As manufacturers were forced to compete and differentiate themselves from their rivals through memorable branding, so railways fetching and carrying these goods felt a similar imperative.

The 1881 Trademark Act made a significant visual impact on US railroads as draftsmen got to work on new insignia. That same year the Chicago, Burlington & Quincy registered the first railroad trademark, a distinctive rectangle enclosing the legend "Burlington Route" created by Daniel Lord of the pioneering

Among the earliest signs to appear on US rolling stock were the builders' plates. Sand-cast in brass or iron, they give the date the locomotive was built, its serial number, or its number in the fleet. They perpetuate the names of the most prolific engine builders: Lima, Baldwin, and Alco.

Chicago advertising agency Lord & Thomas. Lord's logo stayed firmly in place on Burlington Route trains until the Chicago, Burlington & Quincy merged with three other railroads in 1970 to form the Burlington Northern.

Also in 1881 the Union Pacific abandoned its antique-looking mountain elk symbol that might have belonged to any number of western railroads in favor of a distinctive shield design invented by its passenger agent Edward L. Lomax. With a number of subtle changes – among them the adoption of the colors of the US flag in 1888 and Futura-style lettering in the 1940s – this has stayed much the same ever since. Lomax said that it took him a year and a hundred sketches to find the exact right design.

PASSENGER TRAIN SCHEDULES
BETWEEN
CHICAGO AND THE PACIFIC NORTHWEST

PASSENGER TRAIN SCHEDULES
BETWEEN
CHICAGO AND THE PACIFIC NORTHWEST

GREAT NORTHERN RAILWAY

GREAT NORTHERN RAILWAY

MAY 26, 1963
WESTERN STAR

MAY 26, 1963
EMPIRE BUILDER

SEE NEXT PAGE FOR
DAYLIGHT SAVING TIME
INFORMATION

Right: In Walter L. Greene's 1926 poster for the New York Central Lines, the *20th Century Limited* – so called because it stopped at only a limited number of stations – speeds through the Hudson River Valley on its way from New York to Chicago.

By 1883, the Pennsylvania Railroad had begun using its famous and long-lived keystone emblem, a visual reference to the state's nickname The Keystone State. By this time, the Pennsy was not just the largest US railroad, but the world's biggest corporation. The Baltimore & Ohio offered a white-on-blue image of the dome of the US Capitol entwined with the letters B and O encircled by the legend All Trains Run Via Washington.

The Santa Fe's cross-in-a-circle logo, allegedly created in 1880 by J. J. Byrne, the railway's traffic manager, toying creatively with a pen and a silver dollar, was adopted in 1901, while the Great Northern's Rocky Mountain goat trademark leapt from the mind of the railroad's then Vice President W. P. Kenney in 1921. The Great Northern had played a key role in founding the Glacier National Park, where Rocky Mountain goats were a familiar sight. The beaver pelt trademark of

the Rock Island – Chicago, Rock Island & Pacific Railroad – emerged in adverts in 1900 and had been refined into a well-known and enduring logo within five years.

As early as 1890, Edward O. McCormick, the general passenger agent of the Big Four system – the Cleveland, Cincinnati, Chicago & St. Louis Railway formed from a merger of four railroads in 1889 – gave a talk on railway advertising. "Have a trade mark and use it," he said. "Use it every-where… put it on your freight cars and plaster it wherever you can. People will unconsciously learn it, and will recognise it wherever it may be."

As US railroads – many, but not all – abandoned picturesque crests and Gothic lettering in favor of a new generation of trademark emblems with instant visual impact, so they entered an era of speed and style prompted in no small degree by the Chicago World's Fair of 1893. Directors of the Northern Pacific, excited by the look of the

Korean flag which they saw at the fair, adopted a distinctive Yin-Yang logo for their railroad, representing dynamic forces working in harmony and alluding to the company's trade across the North Pacific to the Far East.

The 1893 show also prompted the Pennsylvania and New York Central railroads to speed up their services between New York and Chicago. During the months of the fair, the NYC claimed a 112½ m.p.h. record between Batavia and Buffalo for their high-stepping 4-4-0 locomotive 999 built specially for their accelerated *Empire State Express*. This, though, was a case of fake n.ews dreamed up by over-excited newshounds. The maximum speed was probably no more than 81 mph. However fast it went, 999 made news headlines. This is exactly what George H. Daniels, the NYC's chief public relations officer, had wanted when he proposed a new locomotive design capable of exceeding 100 m.p.h. At a time when the automobile barely existed and the Wright Brothers were still a decade away from successful powered flight, an advance of this order underlined the technological and financial supremacy of the major railroads. Once in Chicago, visitors were exhorted to travel on westward to the Pacific coast on Class I railroads snaking out north, south, and center-west from the Windy City.

From 1911, Class I railroads were defined as those with an annual operating revenue in excess of $1 million. Class II were regional railroads and Class III local lines with a revenue below $100,000. The Class I railroads, ablaze with corporate emblems, backed by ever more creative advertising, underpinned by excellent and robust engineering, and financially sound, reached their zenith in passenger mileage between 1893 and 1916. Even today the US railroad network is the world's largest in terms of operating length. What has gone, for the most part and notably in the great land mass between east and west coasts, is the passenger train, its role usurped from the mid-1950s by the automobile and airplane, both supported by government-subsidized interstate freeways and airports. This, though, was American progress. Mile-long run freight trains, meanwhile, continue to thunder on by, and profitably so, from the Atlantic to the Pacific coasts.

Setting a Style

Like logos, the typefaces that railroad companies used on their rolling stock reinforced their visual identity. Prior to the 1930s, Roman type, with its pronounced serifs, curled legs, and ball terminals, was the standard, reflecting the elegance of railroad travel and the craftmanship with which the trains were built. Until the mid-20th century, the Pullman Car Company used a serif font colloquially referred to as Railroad Roman on the cars it built for Union Pacific, the Santa Fe, and the Baltimore & Ohio. Although this was the most widely used typeface, it was by no means universal; the Pennsylvania Railroad used Clarendon, another serif face.

Right: In 1916, the Pullman Company issued *The Sign Painter*, a distance-learning manual that shared the lettering styles and design principles of the firm's paint shops with "men and boys who wish to better their position by entering the sign painting business, that promises big cash results for those who have energy and pluck."

A historic Union Pacific American-type steam locomotive, built by the Baldwin Works in the 1880s, displays its number in an elegant, eye-catching variant of Railroad Roman.

Right: There were many variants of the ubiquitous Railroad Roman. Draftsmen needed to redesign rather than simply rescale the lettering for each context, in order to maintain its visual impact, especially when seen from a distance. The precise details were codified in volumes of technical specifications such as Union Pacific's Common Standard.

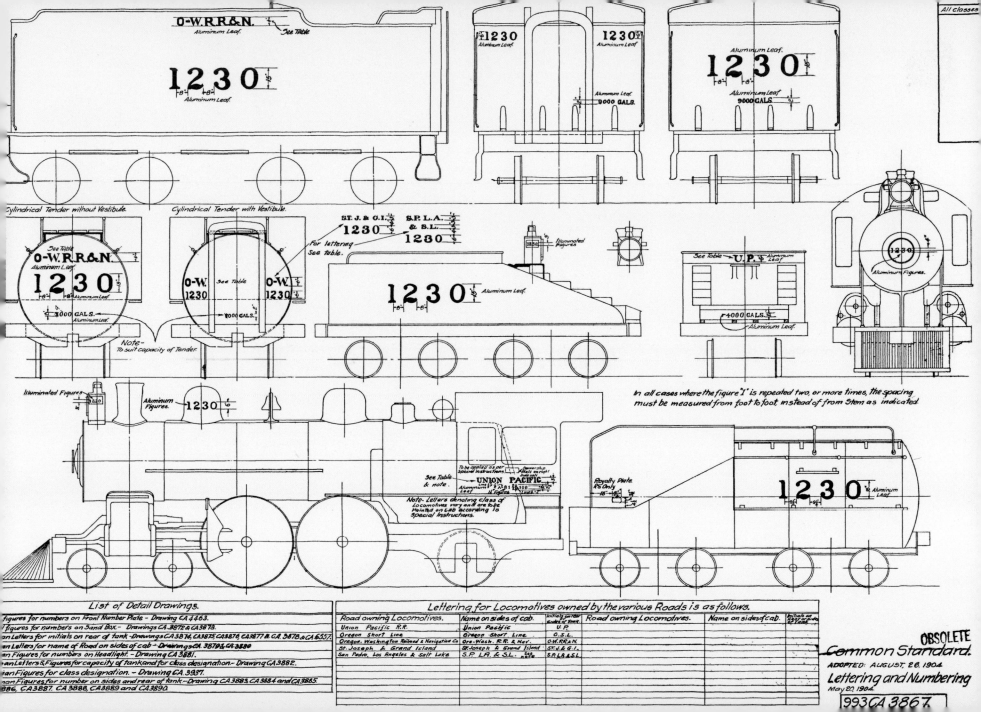

Left: Designs left the engineer's board and entered the paintshop as pounce patterns. The logos, letters, or numbers were drawn onto card, and their outlines perforated with a toothed instrument known as a pounce wheel. The card was taped to the vehicle and chalk dust blown through the holes to leave a guide for the painters, who would then fill in the letters and patterns by hand, as these artisans are doing in Pullman's Detroit shops around 1870.

Above: Graphics could also be put on with stencils of the type stored in the Santa Fe paint shop at Albuquerque. The painters used spray guns or brushes, like these men applying the Burlington Route logo to a boxcar in 1948.

Overland Brands

The logos of the great transcontinental lines – Union Pacific's shield, Santa Fe's cross, the Pennsy's keystone, and Missouri Pacific's red buzzsaw – were generally bold and simple, projecting an image of confidence, competence, and strength.

Burlington Route

Cotton Belt Route

THE MILWAUKEE ROAD

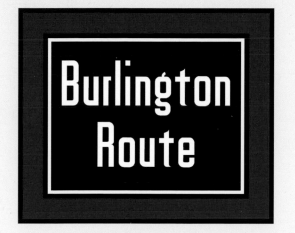

NORTHERN PACIFIC
YELLOWSTONE PARK LINE

PRR

SOUTHERN PACIFIC
LINES

Spirit of the Union

The Union Pacific was founded in 1862 following an Act of Congress approved by Abraham Lincoln to strengthen the Union during the Civil War. Running west from Council Bluffs, Iowa, it met up with the Central Pacific heading east from Sacramento at Promontory Summit, Utah. The year was 1869, and this was the first transcontinental railroad.

From its early years, the Union Pacific proudly called itself The Overland Route. Its eye-catching Armour Yellow and vermillion livery was introduced in 1934 and is seen *(right)* on an 8,500 h.p. X-18 Gas Turbine Electric Locomotive (GTEL) built in 1960.

Above and right: The famous shield and Armour Yellow livery on Union Pacific boxcars bring a splash of color to a freight yard.

Romance of the Southwest

Established in 1859, the Atchison, Topeka & Santa Fe Railway (AT&SF) ran from Kansas to New Mexico, and was extended to Los Angeles in 1887. Ironically, the main line never passed through Santa Fe itself, which was served by a branch; but the romance of New Mexico's pueblo country was a distinctive feature of the railroad's advertising. The Santa Fe ceased operating passenger trains in 1971, and merged with the Burlington Northern in 1995.

The Santa Fe's circle-and-cross motif, used in its original form on a luggage trolley at Albuquerque Station, was elongated to adorn the noses of a range of diesel locomotives, from a GP 30 belching its way through Holbrook, Arizona to the E1 *Super Chief* on a vintage postcard.

Santa Fe GP 35 diesel locomotive 3255 stands among boxcars at Hobart Yard, Los Angeles. The distinctive dark blue and yellow livery, known as Billboard, was introduced in 1960. Only a photographer with a special pass could get an up-close shot like this.

Right: Santa Fe GPs line up at the fueling base in Hobart Yard. The railroad's striking font, with its artisanal-looking rounded serifs, is a variant of Cooper Black.

Santa Fe's herald, seen here on a boxcar and caboose at Richmond, California, was one of the longest-lasting railroad logos, remaining in use for ninety-five years. Company publications state that the passenger traffic manager J. J. Byrne was aboard a train when the idea occurred to him, and that he used a silver dollar to trace the circle. Custom lettering was applied to the shock control boxcars introduced in the 1960s.

Mountain Mascot

Although the Great Northern was absorbed into the Burlington Northern in 1970, its goat mascot still stood proudly on these boxcars in Kansas City when Ian Logan visited a few years later.

The only transcontinental railroad built without federal funding, the Great Northern was constructed between 1857 and 1887, from Minneapolis-St. Paul through Montana and North Dakota to Seattle. The Rocky Mountain goat logo was suggested in 1921 by its Vice President William Kenney, inspired by the billy goat that hauled his newspaper delivery cart when he was a boy.

A Mighty Good Road

The Chicago, Rock Island & Pacific Railroad ran from 1852 to 1980 and was universally known as the Rock Island Lines. The folk song about the railroad was recorded by Lead Belly in the early 1940s and made famous in the UK by Lonnie Donegan.

The Rock Island's beaver-pelt logo *(left)* dated back to the turn of the century but could still be seen forty years later *(right)* adorning the nose cone of a sleek EMD E6 diesel locomotive hauling the *Rocky Mountain Rocket*. This crimson, maroon, and stainless-steel express carried passengers between Chicago and Denver from 1939 to 1966.

ROCKY MOUNTAIN ROCKET
At the Foot of Famous Pikes Peak

The rarely seen motto 100 Years of Progress, surviving here on the side of a rusty boxcar, was photographed by Ian Logan in Kansas City in the 1970s.

100 Years
1852 **Rock Island** 1952
of Progress

EXW   10-4   H   13-8
EW   9-4   H   14-5
IL   40-6

THE
MILWAUKEE
ROAD

Route of
the Super Dome
HIAWATHAS
and Western "CITIES"
Streamliners

ELECTRIFIED OVER THE MOUNTAINS

Olympian

THE MILWAUKEE ROAD

The Milwaukee Road was quick to grasp the marketing potential of giving memorable names to its long-distance passenger trains. The *Olympian* came into service in 1911, just two years after the Pacific extension was completed, and the line was electrified between 1915 and 1927. Its fleet of streamlined *Hiawathas* – named after the hero of Longfellow's poem – followed in 1935.

Southern Blues

The railroads that ran up the Mississippi River formed the main artery of African-American migration from the cotton fields of the South to the cities of the Midwest and the Great Lakes. Their iconography reflected this contradictory heritage: the Gulf Mobile & Ohio ran trains named *Abraham Lincoln* on its northern lines and *The Rebel* in the South, while the St. Louis Southwestern embraced its post-slavery nickname, the Cotton Belt Route. Sonny Boy Williamson's song "GM&O Blues," recorded in Chicago in 1945, captures both the liberation and the melancholy of the long journey north.

Created by the merger of the Gulf, Mobile & Northern Railroad and the Mobile & Ohio Railroad in 1938, the Gulf Mobile & Ohio – popularly known as the GeeMo – sported a distinctive winged logo, seen here on a General Motors GP 38 diesel-electric locomotive and a woven badge.

Formed in 1875 as the Tyler Tap Railroad, the St. Louis Southwestern ran passenger trains from St. Louis to Texas and from Memphis to Dallas, retaining its identity after it became a subsidiary of Southern Pacific in 1932. Its distinctive Cotton Belt herald, deployed on locomotives, boxcars, timetables, and onboard menus, was designed by a Mr. Charles Ware in the mid-1880s, and based on a cross-section of a cotton gin.

The Illinois Central's old lozenge-shaped herald was replaced in 1966 by the robust initial i, shaped like a rail in cross-section, that appears on this caboose. In 1972 the railroad was merged with the Gulf Mobile & Ohio to form the Illinois Central Gulf.

ILLINOIS CENTRAL

Main Line of Mid-America

The DIAMOND MATCH CO., CHICAGO, ILL.

Multiple Identities

On any network as vast as that of the US, trains made up of boxcars belonging to different railroads were a common sight, resulting in a profusion of logos and typography in freight yards across the land.

Boxcars of the Santa Fe and Central of Georgia stand alongside a cushioned freight wagon of the Cotton Belt (St. Louis Southwestern Railway) in Los Angeles.

Overleaf: Boxcars of the Southern Pacific and Rock Island Lines stand cheek by jowl in the freight yards at Kansas City.

SOUTHERN
PACIFIC
EXW 10-8 H 12-11
EW 9-10 H 14
IL 50-6
IW 9-3
IH 10-4
CU FT 4836
BLT. 1-69 B-70-41

ROCK ISLAND
R. I.
33342
CAPY 149000 A-220
LD LMT 144100
LT WT 75900 BK. 5.74
DF 2

2. A SENSE OF PLACE

From small beginnings in the 19th century, a clutch of railroad empires extended north, south, east, and west without ever reaching from coast to coast. Some snaked out to connect distant cities, others developed or acquired a dense network of lines within a particular region, while a few grew to cover many states. Despite their expansion, many never forgot their geographical origins, preserving home-town names and symbols in their branding. The stories of these very different railways and the way they chose to present themselves to their public are as rich and varied as the landscape of the United States.

The Norfolk & Western, for example, began life in 1838 as the City Point Rail Road, a nine-mile short line connecting Petersburg, Virginia and the docks at City Point. In 1854 it was absorbed into the South Side Railroad between Petersburg and Lynchburg. The Norfolk & Petersburg Railroad, meanwhile, was completed in 1858. Both the South Side and the N&P were wrecked in the Civil War. Afterwards they merged with the Virginia & Tennessee Railroad to create the Atlantic, Mississippi & Ohio Railroad (AM&O), which was renamed the Norfolk & Western in 1881 and continued its westward expansion into the 1970s when, after some 200 mergers, it had extended its reach as far as Kansas City and St. Louis. With its headquarters and workshops at Roanoke, Virginia, however, the Norfolk & Western remained firmly rooted in the state of its birth.

The Louisville & Nashville, founded in 1850, took nine long years to reach its terminus at Nashville. An inter-city railroad crossing the Kentucky-Tennessee border, the L&N was used by both sides in the Civil War, and suffered extensive damage. It recovered quickly, however, and then just kept growing, steaming out to St. Louis, Atlanta, and New Orleans, its lines reaching into fourteen states by the time of World War I. But it remained resolutely the Louisville & Nashville.

Until the companies that came to own it were finally swallowed up by mergers in the 1980s, the matter-of-fact L&N emblem displayed on the tenders and noses of steam and diesel locomotives stayed pretty much the same decade after decade. The capital letters L&N framed in a rectangle were gradually simplified and even sloped

POWERED BY PEOPLE

NORFOLK AND WESTERN RAILWAY

Opened in 1891, the Manitou and Pikes Peak Railway used a rack or cog system to reach the 14,114-foot summit in Colorado. It is the highest cog railway in the world.

forward in later years to reflect a new age of speed, yet the L&N seemed little influenced by fashion.

Other railroads that might have grown from small beginnings are little more than a memory today. Incorporated in 1883, the Colorado Midland was the first standard-gauge railway to make the epic crossing of the Rocky Mountains in Colorado. Heroically, it climbed 130 miles from Colorado Springs (elevation 6,035 feet) to Leadville (elevation 10,152 feet). Tight curves, long tunnels, and arduous gradients as steep as one in twenty-five witnessed Colorado Midland trains pounding up into winter snows headed by some of the most powerful US locomotives in service at the time.

Not surprisingly, this was a difficult line to operate with geography, topography, and climate presenting formidable challenges. When during World War I the federal government diverted essential heavy freight trains over the Midland Route – a legend witnessed in some versions of the railway's simple logo – the infrastructure

was unable to cope. Instead of bringing prosperity to the Colorado Midland, this extra long-distance work brought about its premature demise in 1918.

One version of this short-lived railroad's emblem, a black, red, and white roundel encircling the outline of a pyramid with an illustration of a mountaintop within, displayed the name Pikes Peak Route. While the track bed of the line from Colorado Springs to Leadville became a highway, US Route 24, in the 1920s, the Pikes Peak Cog Railway survived, climbing to the top of the peak from 1891 to 2017. It is about to be rebuilt for the future and, if everything goes to plan, will reopen in the early 2020s.

While natural landscapes featured in a number of railroad trademarks and emblems, others were more abstract. The Wabash, a Midwestern line joining the Great Lakes to St. Louis, Kansas City, and Buffalo, adopted a partially unfurled red banner in 1886 and called itself The Banner Line of the Central States. Later the banner became a flag emblem, which by 1912 had morphed into one bearing the legend Follow the Flag. The flag had fallen by 1964, when the Wabash was leased by the Norfolk & Western Railway, to be fully absorbed into their corporate structure later.

Rather than flag waving, the Georgia Railroad & Banking Company, operating between Athens, Augusta, and Atlanta, adapted the State of Georgia seal with an emblem featuring a classical portico. One column reads Courtesy, another Service, while Safety is a banner hung between the two. The portico's architrave is emblazoned with the words Old Reliable. More reliable than the finances of the railway were

those of the banking arm. Nevertheless, their trains and locomotives bore this trademark into the early 1980s when the Georgia lost its identity and very nearly all its surviving freight trains.

Many American railroads tended to ride a financial roller coaster throughout their lives. So, suggesting financial security through a name and logo must have seemed a good idea, as it certainly was to the New York, Chicago & St. Louis, which adopted the nickname The Nickel Plate Road. They picked up the idea from a congratulatory newspaper report. One of four railways competing for traffic through northern Ohio, they had sent surveyors to Norwalk in March 1881 in preparation, wrote F. R. Loomis, editor of the *Norwalk Chronicle*, for the "great New York and St. Louis double track, nickel plate road." The name stuck. Loomis was rewarded with the railroad's Complimentary Pass No. 1, and New York, Chicago & St. Louis rolling stock bore the name Nickel Plate Road in saloon bar script until 1964 when they became a part of the Norfolk & Western's fleet.

Some US railroads were so distinctive that emblems, trademarks, and logos would have made little difference to the way they were perceived or their fortunes fluctuated. The Sacramento Northern was truly a railroad apart, running electric trains from 1918 over the 183 miles from Chico via Sacramento to Oakland, California, threading along city streets where necessary. Cracking along at up to 60 m.p.h., the Sacramento electrics offered dining and observation cars as they insinuated their way through majestic landscapes, the name of the railroad spelt out on the sides of locomotives and carriages in elementary lettering.

In its heyday, the 522-mile Florida East Coast main line from Jacksonville to Miami and Key West was one of the most glamorous of all regional railways. Its new insurance company-style logo evokes none of the colorful history and compelling seaboard scenery of a railroad built to serve new-build hotels and a burgeoning holiday business, to say nothing of the improbable crossing over twenty-two miles of open water and at least two dozen bridges to Key West, just ninety miles north of Havana.

The Florida East Coast Railway was the creation of one man, Henry Flagler. Retired from Standard Oil, where he made his fortune,

Flagler not only promoted and built the railway but, in the process, invented Miami and modern Florida. What started off in the public imagination as a mosquito- and alligator-infested swamp had by 1912, when the railroad reached Key West, become the acme of sun-kissed glamor. The Key West extension was destroyed by a 200-m.p.h. hurricane in 1935, yet the romance of the line was not washed away with it. Its trains reached their zenith in speed and design in 1939 with the launch of diesel-powered expresses in a bright red and yellow livery. They were embellished with a sunshine-motif logo that had evolved over time in the railway's advertising department. Livery and logo have reappeared on diesel freight locomotives operating the line today.

From 1926, Miami could also be reached from Jacksonville by trains of the Seaboard Air Line Railroad – "air line" was a 19th-century expression for the shortest distance between two points. The line rode down through west and central Florida before heading for the Atlantic coast. Its fast olive green, orange, and cream diesel trains carried a logo encircling a heart and the message,

An early Florida East Coast logo adorns the company's ticket office in the Ingraham Building in downtown Miami. The Long Key Viaduct formed the centerpiece of the design until its destruction in 1935.

Through the Heart of the South. This eye-catching design had emerged from earlier devices dreamed up by railroad staff. Its boxcars displayed stylized handwriting declaring Route of the *Orange Blossom Special*.

Some of the more obscure rural railroads steamed on remarkably late into the day. In 1955, Walt Disney decided to make a film about the famous Civil War railway chase between Union spies and Southern railwaymen along the Western & Atlantic Railroad between Atlanta and Chattanooga. Disney chose another obscure Georgia railway as the set for his re-telling of the story. With its forest settings, numerous trestle bridges, and vintage atmosphere, the 57-mile Tallulah Falls Railway, crossing the border between North Carolina and Georgia, proved to be an ideal location. Its principal attraction to visitors was the Tallulah Gorge with its cascade of six waterfalls dubbed the Niagara of the South. A railroad enthusiast, Disney tried to buy the route when closure threatened. Its owners, Southern Railway, turned him down. They abandoned the line in 1961. This was a decidedly "no logo" operation, its name spelt out in workaday lettering only, and yet the Tallulah Falls could hardly have been a less singular or romantic railway.

Images of the Wild West, banners, snowy peaks, and antebellum classical porticos would have seemed out of place for the busy commuter lines fingering out from New York, Boston, Philadelphia, Chicago, and Los Angeles. Searching for a telling alternative, one such railway came up with something very different indeed. Among the busiest of US railways, the Long Island Rail Road, formed in

An 1898 poster by J. P. Beckwith highlights the Florida East Coast Railway's role in developing the state as a Paradise Regained for sun-seekers from the north.

Florida East Coast Railway

The East Coast of Florida is Paradise Regained.

Florida East Coast Steamship Co.
Key West-Miami Line
Miami-Nassau Line

1834, was and is very much a passenger line. Between 1959 and 1967 its frequent trains heading in and out of Manhattan were decorated with decals depicting Dan the Dashing Commuter. Willfully folksy, the logo was based on a doodle by Bill Mallory of the Long Island's three-man PR department, which paid a cartoonist $10 to "shake it up." "We're damn amateur," said PR Chief Jim Schultz as Dashing Dan raced into public view, first for promotional use in the *Long Island Railroader* newspaper and then on the sides of trains. Like many US railroads, the Long Island felt quite comfortable developing its own style in-house, even when in its case there were dozens of highly regarded advertising agencies and design studios close by ready and willing to tell the railroads what they should be doing to attract customers.

In recent decades, as most US railways have lost their individual identities, slick, stylized logos from design studios have come to rule the roost. For much of their history, though, many US railroads, from short lines to Class I giants, proudly proclaimed their local roots in homespun imagery and words.

Pride in their Roots

While many railroads that started small grew into major carriers, their geographic origins still defined their imagery. Some logos featured local heroes, such as the Boston & Maine's Minuteman; others symbols like the Northwestern Pacific's giant redwood.

"Follow the Flag"

Maritime and Coastal

The earliest railroads in the US all ran along the eastern seaboard, connecting coastal cities such as Boston, New York, Baltimore, Washington, Richmond, and Jacksonville. Negotiating inlets, creeks, and islands along the way, many were closely involved with maritime activities. In 1912, the Florida East Coast Railway completed its Over-Sea Railroad, a long series of viaducts which extended its line to Key West, the closest deep-water port in the US to the Panama Canal. On the West Coast, railroads like the Western Pacific operated fleets of tugboats to ferry freight cars across San Francisco harbor.

The Atlantic Coast Line was formed in 1893 following the mergers of several local lines. Its roundel, seen here on a piggy-back trailer at the 60th Street Yard, New York was in use from 1910 and instantly recognizable by its flamboyant wavy serifs.

The Western Pacific's distinctive feather motif adorns the funnel of the steam tug *Hercules* in San Francisco harbor.

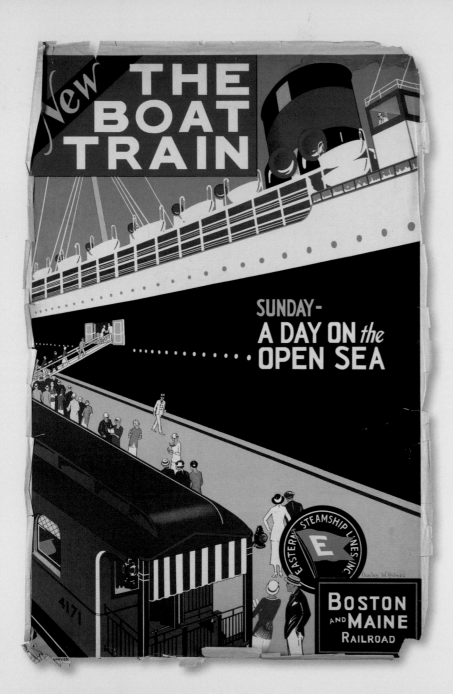

Chartered in 1835, the Boston & Maine branded its rolling stock with a simple typographic logo in a plain oblong frame. In 1945, the railroad introduced a new herald featuring a Minuteman from the American Revolution *(right)*. These were members of the local militia who promised to be available to fight at a minute's notice. During the first battle of the war in 1775, they were, forcing the British Army to withdraw at Lexington, Massachusetts.

Left: A 1920s excursion poster by the artist Charles W. Holmes makes the most of the Boston & Maine's maritime connections.

A new Boston & Maine logo by the designer Herbert Matter was introduced in 1956. On a locomotive at Gorham, New Hampshire it has been painted over the old Minuteman herald.

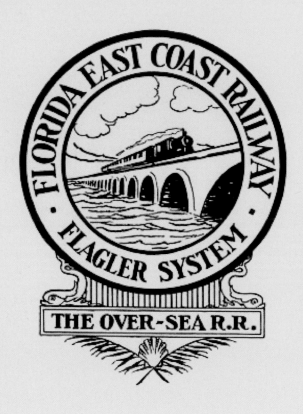

A Pineapple Special on Long Key Viaduct, F. E. C. Ry., Jacksonville, Fla.

Henry M. Flagler, the founder of Miami, created the Florida East Coast Railway (FEC) in 1895 after buying up a number of local lines. The company's Over-Sea Railroad through the Florida Keys extended the line over a series of viaducts like the one at Long Key above.

Right: Like the FEC, the rival Seaboard Air Line Railroad emphasized the subtropical allure of Florida; from 1939 to 1953 the EMD diesel locomotives of its Orange Blossom Special service were painted in bright citrus colors.

The Orange Blossom Special Going Through Orange Groves in Florida

The classic Florida East Coast logo,
in use from 1936 to 1960, evokes the
state's holiday climate with an idyllic
vista of sea, sun, and palm trees.

The Seaboard Air Line Railroad ran from Richmond, Virginia to Miami until 1967, when it merged with the Atlantic Coast Line to form the Seaboard Coast Line.

California's beachside attractions featured prominently in promotional photographs for Southern Pacific's Suntan Special, inaugurated in 1927 to take holidaymakers from San Jose to the resorts of Monterey Bay. When the service was resumed in 1947 after its suspension during World War II, it was greeted by large crowds at Casino Station in Santa Cruz. An SP subsidiary, the Northwestern Pacific Railroad, was opened in 1914 to transport lumber from northern California, and its logo, painted *(right)* on a San Francisco harbor tugboat, alluded to the coastal redwoods through which it ran.

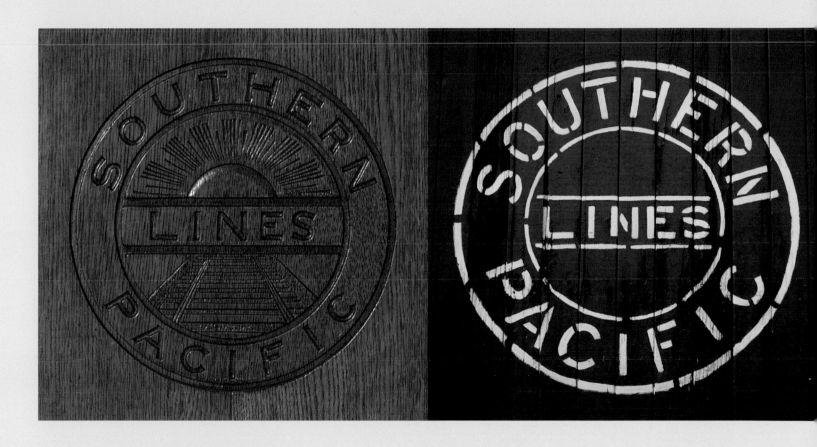

The Southern Pacific's bold sunrise logo could be
applied to a variety of surfaces, whether painted on
the side of a company truck, branded into the wood of
a bench in San Francisco station, or stenciled onto a
freight car.

Chicago and the Lakes

Chicago's location at the southern tip of Lake Michigan and the edge of the Midwest made it the hub for many railroads, both transcontinental and those that, like the Chicago & Eastern Illinois, served the Great Lakes area. Chartered in 1859, the Chicago & North Western operated more than 10,000 miles of track at its peak, carrying potatoes, wheat, and corn from the prairies. It was taken over by Union Pacific in 1995.

Left: Stenciled onto a steam locomotive tender, the logo of the Chicago & Illinois Midland Railway, a little known short line, is a no-nonsense affair.

Right: The herald of the Chicago & North Western, extant for more than a century, was known as the "ball and bar."

THE WABASH RAILWAY

Is the Best and Most Popular Route running Through Cars between
the following principal points:

ST. LOUIS AND

TOLEDO,   ROCHESTER,

DETROIT,   BUFFALO,

ST. THOMAS,   NEW YORK
                                   AND
NIAGARA FALLS,   BOSTON.

CHICAGO AND

ST. LOUIS,   HANNIBAL

PEORIA,   *AND*

QUINCY,   KANSAS CITY.

TOLEDO AND QUINCY.

DETROIT AND QUINCY.

*KEOKUK TO INDIANAPOLIS
AND CINCINNATI.*

The Through Car Service is unrivaled, and consists of

Elegant Free Reclining Chair Cars.

Pullman, Wagner and Woodruff Sleeping Cars.

THE DINING CAR SERVICE

Is the very best, and unsurpassed by any other road.

For Tickets, Routes, Rates, Maps, Folders and full information,
call on or address any Agent of the Wabash Railway or connecting lines.

S. W. SNOW,
General Passenger Agent,
CHICAGO.

Taking its name from a tributary of the Ohio River, the Wabash Railroad arose from a series of mergers from 1865 onwards. It connected Rochester, Buffalo, Detroit, and Chicago with Kansas City, St. Louis, De Moines, and Omaha – from where the Union Pacific continued to the West Coast. Its first logo, seen on this 1887 timetable (left), was a red scroll bearing the words The Wabash Railway.

Right: The Wabash herald soon developed into a flag, believed to refer to the one carried by an engine that would run down the track the day before the pay car was due. The motto Follow the Flag was added in 1912.

"Follow the Flag"

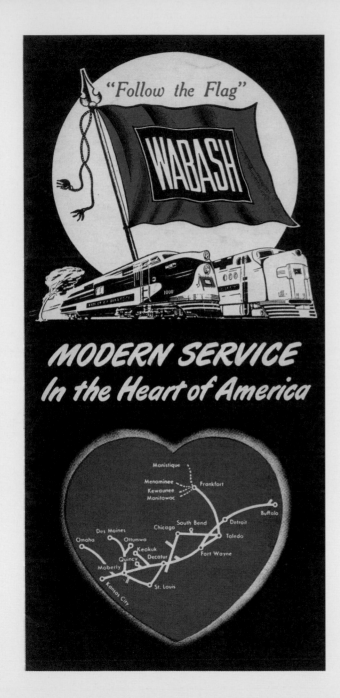
"WABASH CANNON BALL"

SAVES YOU HOURS BETWEEN THE SOUTHWEST AND DETROIT!

Shortest, fastest rail route between Detroit and major Southwestern cities! You make direct connections at St. Louis Union Station with excellent trains to and from Texas and Oklahoma—no crosstown transfer! The fine modern *Wabash Cannon Ball* offers observation-parlor car service, reclining seat coaches, superb dining car meals, Diesel power.

For tickets and reservations, see your agent or call the nearest Wabash representative listed on Page 1 of this timetable.

SOUTHBOUND Read Down		"WABASH CANNON BALL"	NORTHBOUND Read Up	
7:35 A.M.	Lv.	Detroit (EST)	Ar.	8:55 P.M.
5:05 P.M.	Ar.	St. Louis Union Station (CST)	Lv.	9:00 A.M.

CONNECTING TRAIN SERVICE

"TEXAS EAGLE" MISSOURI PACIFIC

5:30 P.M.	Lv.	St. Louis Union Station	Ar.	8:20 A.M.
7:30 A.M.	Ar.	Dallas Union Station	Lv.	6:15 P.M.
8:30 A.M.	Ar.	Fort Worth	Lv.	5:15 P.M.
10:00 A.M.	Ar.	Houston	Lv.	4:00 P.M.
10:00 A.M.	Ar.	Austin	Lv.	3:43 P.M.
11:40 A.M.	Ar.	San Antonio	Lv.	2:10 P.M.

"TEXAS SPECIAL" FRISCO-MKT

5:30 P.M.	Lv.	St. Louis Union Station	Ar.	8:10 A.M.
7:30 A.M.	Ar.	Dallas Union Station	Lv.	6:10 P.M.
7:35 A.M.	Ar.	Fort Worth	Lv.	5:10 P.M.
9:50 A.M.	Ar.	Waco	Lv.	4:00 P.M.
12:01 P.M.	Ar.	Austin	Lv.	1:42 P.M.
1:55 P.M.	Ar.	San Antonio	Lv.	12:01 P.M.

"METEOR" FRISCO

7:00 P.M.	Lv.	St. Louis Union Station	Ar.	7:45 A.M.
5:30 A.M.	Ar.	Tulsa	Lv.	9:45 P.M.
8:25 A.M.	Ar.	Oklahoma City	Lv.	7:00 P.M.

(All Trains Daily)

Over the decades the folk song "The Wabash Cannon Ball", about a mythical train, was recorded by Roy Acuff, the Carter Family, Woody Guthrie, Earl Scruggs, Pete Seeger, and others. The name Cannon Ball was given to trains from 1888 when a Wabash timetable displayed an express being fired from a cannon and continued into the diesel age *(left)*.

Opened in 1884, the Minneapolis, St. Paul & Sault Ste. Marie Railroad was popularly known as the Soo Line, after the pronunciation of Sault in the name of the US-Canadian border town. On its merger with two other railroads in 1961, Soo became its official name, displayed on everything from locomotives to matchbooks.

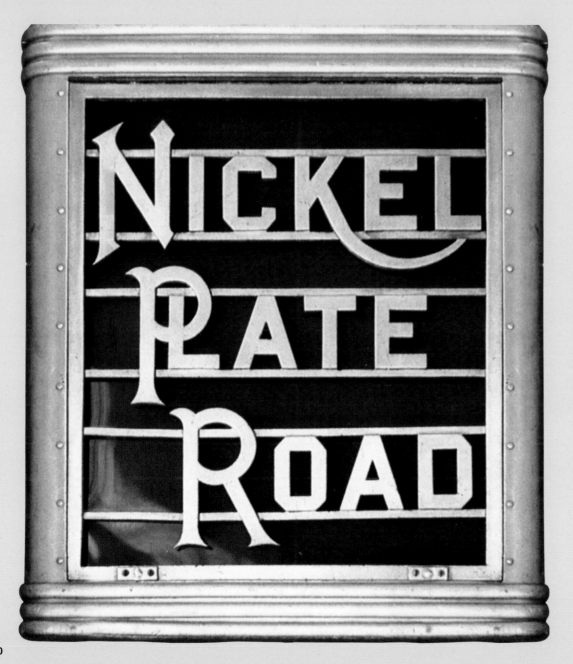

Established in 1881, the New York, Chicago & St. Louis Railroad Company did much to stimulate the economic growth of the areas it passed through. When the *Norwalk Chronicle* called it a "double track, nickel plated railroad," the name stuck, and was soon adopted by the company itself.

Left: The Nickel Plate Road's stylized lettering, designed in 1917, gets a stylish Art Deco treatment on this passenger-car drumhead.

The classic Nickel Plate font was printed prominently on timetables, advertisements, and employee passes. By linking up with the Lackawanna Railroad, the company was able to extend its services to New Jersey.

Southern Connections

Some of the first US railroads were established in the South. The Central of Georgia began life as the Central Rail Road and Banking Company of Georgia in 1833. The Georgia Railroad opened the following year. Originally connecting Athens to Augusta, it soon extended to Atlanta, where it linked up with other lines to Charleston and Memphis. The Louisville & Nashville was a relative newcomer, inaugurated in 1850. All suffered during the Civil War, which was mostly fought in the South: in 1864, Union troops sabotaged the Central's tracks by bending the rails into loops they called "Sherman's neckties." But most recovered and prospered, continuing to expand until the amalgamations of the 1960s and 1970s.

Left: A railway worker checks a Louisville & Nashville freight car in snowy St. Louis. The Chase Bag Co. in the background made cotton bags for transporting flour. The L&N inherited the Dixie Line nickname from the Nashville, Chattanooga & St. Louis Railway, which it took over in 1957.

The Louisville & Nashville was one of the most extensive networks in the South. It continued to run freight and passenger services until it was taken over by the Seaboard Coast Line Railroad in 1971, the year after Ian Logan photographed this bay-window caboose in Kansas City.

The classical columns of the Georgia Railroad logo echo the antebellum architecture of the Deep South, and proclaim old-fashioned virtues.

Left: The Georgia Railroad's neoclassical portico adorns the nose of an EMD F3 (A) locomotive at Decatur, Georgia.

The Central of Georgia retained its logo even after its absorption by the Southern Railway in 1963. On this caboose, its crisp typography is offset by the flowing script and long tail of the slogan The Right Way.

Commuter Lines

At the opposite end of the spectrum from the "lonesome whistle" of a transcontinental train crossing the prairies were the busy urban lines that shuttled commuters between their homes and workplaces five days a week. While long-distance and regional passenger rail services have all but disappeared from the United States, commuter transit systems still carry millions of passengers a day. Among the largest and busiest are the Massachusetts Bay Transportation Authority, the Long Island Rail Road, and the Metrolink, which serve the suburbs of Boston, New York, and Los Angeles respectively.

Here She Is: Dashing Dottie!

Meet Dashing Dottie!

You're getting a preview introduction. Dottie will make her public debut tomorrow —in the latest issue of **Dashing Dan's Diary**, which will be aboard all morning trains to the City.

Dottie is the culmination of a dream for a companion for Dan—and the answer to those distaff passengers who've felt left out because of the emphasis on Dan all these years.

While Dan just "growed" from a doodle on a Public Relations Department desk pad, Dottie was carefully "assembled" until the combination of anatomical parts and clothing seemed just right.

There are plenty of projects in which Dottie will figure in the future. She'll start working on the railroad as a prominent part of the design for two handsome new sales items that will be available shortly to both passengers and employes.

One will be a double deck of Congress-quality playing cards, with Dottie on one deck and Dan on the other. Single deck purchasers will be able to choose either Dan or Dottie.

The other item is a really unusual one—a "Dan 'n' Dottie Cocktails for Two" set in a handsome, mailable package.

It'll consist of a 16-ounce Libby glass mixing pitcher, two matching cocktail glasses and a glass stirrer. On one glass will be Dottie; on the other, Dan. Both will be on the pitcher—running headlong at each other.

Cards and cocktails sets will be ready about the end of May. We'll let you know when— and what our rock-bottom prices will be for members of the LIRR family—in a future Railroader.

And, if you have any ideas or suggestions on how Dottie might make appearances, just drop a note to Public Relations, Room 310, Jamaica Station Building.

In the 1950s, as rush-hour traffic grew between Long Island and New York, the Long Island Rail Road's PR department came up with an inventive advertising campaign. Dashing Dan appeared on ticket booths, matchbooks, and other ephemera, while Dashing Dottie was launched in the LIRR magazine. The pair embodied the busy, modern lifestyle of the growing cohort of office workers.

Left: The New York, New Haven & Hartford Railroad ran passenger and freight services throughout southern New England from 1872 to 1968, when it was absorbed into the Penn Central. Its florid Beaux Arts logo was created in the 1890s, and continued in use until 1955, when the designer Herbert Matter replaced it with a Modernist monogram.

Right: The Key System derived its name from the shape formed on a stylized map by its network of electric interurban lines connecting the Bay Area cities of Oakland, Berkeley, and Alameda to San Francisco. The East Bay Transit Company was a subsidiary running streetcars around Oakland.

987

In addition to its long-distance services to the Great Lakes region, the New York Central Railroad operated commuter lines in New York City and Massachusetts. Its EMD E8 passenger-train locomotive is painted Century Green. To the left, a conductor hangs from the side of the its famous passenger train, the *20th Century Limited*.

3. ARRIVALS AND DEPARTURES

An epiphany of clanging bells, chiming whistles, baritone hooters, and the percussive ministry of air-brake pumps announced the arrival of generations of trains at railroad stations across the United States. It was as if religious processions were coming to town. And, in a sense, they were. For the American railroad station or depot was, as medieval parish churches had been in Europe, the ritualistic hub around which life turned, especially in remote settlements.

As trains drew in, stations burst into life. Station wagons, horse-powered before 1900, met passengers and their luggage bound for hotels. The station telegraph would be busy with reports on the line ahead and messages to and from passengers and their points of departure. Freight and baggage were manhandled in and out of boxcars and cabooses.

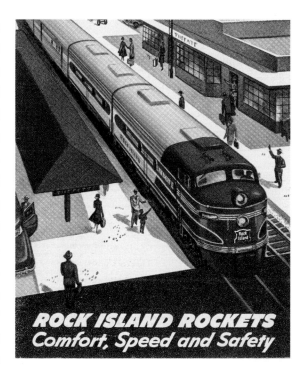

ROCK ISLAND ROCKETS
Comfort, Speed and Safety

Through Westerns and soap operas like *Little House on the Prairie* or the haunting black-and-white photographs of O. Winston Link, a New York advertising man who had fallen hook, line, and chime whistle for that most characterful of US railroads, the Norfolk & Western, in the late 1950s, this railroad ceremony is etched into our collective subconscious. So, too, are the destinations railroads promoted with a missionary verve to populate the new towns, growing cities, and magnificent, if challenging, landscapes they steamed through as they spun their web of steel across the continent.

Many US cities – especially great Midwestern hubs like Chicago, Kansas City, and St. Louis – were not only destinations in their own right, but hubs and transit points for passengers and freight. Often, both would

Through the 1920s and 1930s, railroad companies commissioned superb posters promoting the great cities of the United States as compelling, charismatic destinations. Foremost among the commercial artists working for the New York Central was Leslie Ragan, a World War I airman who created this breathtaking aerial view of New York Harbor in 1935.

require cross-town transport to continue their journey to the East or West Coast from another terminal.

By 1900, American passengers might find themselves boarding or alighting trains at stations designed in the guise of Romanesque abbey churches, Greek temples, imperial Roman baths, Gothic cathedrals, medieval cloth halls, Italianate palazzi, French châteaux, Black Forest gingerbread houses, Spanish missions, and homespun farmsteads. Through this encyclopedia of styles, US railways expressed their values and ambitions. Station design could also be a reflection of local architectural character. Daniel Burnham's mighty Union Station in Washington, DC, opened in 1907, is an equal match for the Neoclassical civic temples and monuments lining the city's National Mall.

For many Americans, the architecture of ancient Greece and Rome embodied republican and democratic virtues. Commanding a vista of streets and avenues fanning out from Columbus Circle, Union Station is fronted by a giant reiteration of the Arch of Constantine. Through this Neo-Roman portal as many as 200,000

LESLIE
RAGAN

NEW YORK THE UPPER BAY FROM LOWER MANHATTAN

NEW YORK CENTRAL SYSTEM

On this 1935 Pennsylvania Railroad poster Grif Teller bathes the Neoclassical architecture of Washington in golden sunlight. The GG1-class electric locomotive in the foreground represented the acme of modern transportation, having come into service the previous year. Nicknamed Old Rivets, it is now preserved at the Railroad Museum of Pennsylvania.

passengers a day have flocked into the Great Hall behind it, the imperious design of which is based on the Baths of Diocletian. "Make no little plans," Burnham said. "They have no magic to stir men's blood."

Because it was a union station – one serving the trains of all trunk railroads entering and leaving major US cities – few visual references were made to the individual railways that had made their home here in the federal capital. Instead of railroad insignia, passengers contemplated allegorical statues representing industry or agriculture and a parade of marble centurions above the arcading of the Great Hall.

In 1981, part of the station's ceiling collapsed. This prompted a renovation whereby much of Burnham's building was transformed into a food court and shopping mall. While the station itself remains busy, passenger numbers are a tenth of what they were at their peak in 1945. It was the remarkable if short-lived success of US railroads, especially in the number of passengers who used them, that prompted the building of prodigious new stations between

The magnificent Pennsylvania Station of 1910 takes center stage in this poster promoting train services to the World's Fair of 1939, held in Flushing Meadows, New York.

1900 and 1940. As passenger numbers tumbled from 1945, with soldiers settling back home and the construction of freeways and airports energized by state subsidies, many of these grandiose monuments faced redundancy and even demolition.

Despite vehement protest by New Yorkers, one of the greatest of all, Pennsylvania Station, was torn down in 1963. Opened in 1910 and linked by tunnels to the east and west of Manhattan, this opulent and much-loved temple to train travel was designed by McKim, Mead & White in the style of the Baths of Caracalla. "Until the first blow fell," reported the *New York Times* on October 30th, 1963, "no one was convinced that Penn Station really would be demolished, or that New York would permit this monumental act of vandalism against one of the largest and finest landmarks of Roman elegance."

The Pennsylvania Railroad, however, had fallen on hard times. The decline of the US passenger train had already brought ambitious and distinctive railway architecture to a halt, but the Pennsy blew it apart. In demolishing Penn Station it planned to

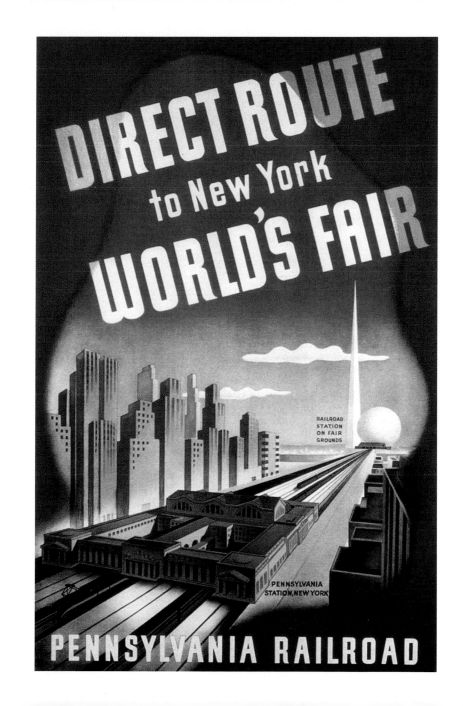

DIRECT ROUTE to New York WORLD'S FAIR

RAILROAD STATION ON FAIR GROUNDS

PENNSYLVANIA STATION, NEW YORK

PENNSYLVANIA RAILROAD

sell air rights above a new underground concourse to property speculators. It did, and the result remains as grim as the day the new station opened in 1964. "One entered the city like a God," said the American architectural historian Vincent Scully of the 1910 station. "One scuttles in now like a rat." Legislators, however, did respond quickly with new laws protecting historic buildings. These were upheld when, unabashed, the Penn Central, a union of the Pennsylvania and New York Central Railroads, attempted to butcher Penn Station's one-time rival, the equally magnificent Grand Central Terminal.

With 44 tracks on two levels and a truly breathtaking main concourse measuring 275 feet long, 120 feet wide, and 125 feet high, lined with Italian marble, lit by vast Roman lunette windows, and covered by a ceiling representing the heavens and their constellations, Grand Central was very grand indeed. Designed by Reed & Stern and Warren & Wetmore for the New York Central and opened in 1913, it faced mutilation in 1968 when a skyscraper by the former Bauhaus architect Marcel Breuer was announced. This

was to have shot up from the innards of the station. The bid failed and, radiantly restored, Grand Central, a National Historic Landmark today, goes about its business in a sublime style airports have been unable even remotely to equal.

One of the most feted and photographed of all US train stations is Point of Rocks, Maryland, a junction on the Potomac River where the Baltimore & Ohio's Washington and Baltimore branches meet. Designed by E. Francis Baldwin, the red brick and sandstone Gothic Revival building opened in 1873. Its tall steeple gives it the look and feel of a rustic church – no surprise since Baldwin was a prolific ecclesiastical architect. Steeples and towers enabled railroads to advertise their presence in a town, visible from a distance and worthy to rub shoulders with the other estates of the realm. Baldwin repeated this theme in Baltimore. His Mount Royal terminus, a solemn Romanesque and Italian Renaissance design crowned with a 150-foot clock tower decorated for many years with the B&O logo, might be mistaken for some grand monastery in the wooded hills of Tuscany. Closed in 1961, Mount Royal has

UNION STATION, ST. LOUIS, MO.

been sympathetically converted into a home for the Maryland Institute College of Art.

Lucius Beebe, the US journalist and railroad historian, described Mount Royal as "one of the celebrated railroad stations of the world, ranking in renown with Euston Station, London, scene of so many Sherlock Holmes' departures, the Gare du Nord in Paris, and the feudal fortress of the Pennsylvania Railroad at Broad Street, Philadelphia." These three stations had been raised in markedly different styles – Greek Revival, Beaux-Arts, and an overwhelming marriage of Gormenghast Gothic and Renaissance Free Style – a reminder that until the triumph of Modern architecture, railway stations around the world were built with exuberant stylistic variety.

One of the best-loved Romanesque stations is Cheyenne Depot, built by the Union Pacific from 1886 to 1888 in the town the railroad

itself had founded 20 years earlier. A true cathedral of the railway age with its ecclesiastical-style clock tower, the sandstone building designed by Henry Van Brunt and Frank Howe is now home to the Cheyenne Depot Museum. From here, visitors are taken to the holy of railroading holies, the Union Pacific Steam Shop, where the railroad's hugely impressive 4-8-4 express passenger locomotive 844 is prepared for special duties and where a wartime Big Boy 4-8-8-4, a colossally powerful and remarkably fast freight locomotive, has recently been restored for main-line running.

Some of the most distinctive stations are to be found along the route of the Atchison, Topeka & Santa Fe Railway heading southwest from Kansas City. In California, it traced a section of the venerable Camino Real, the road between Spanish mission stations. It was these that did much to inspire the Santa Fe's distinctive regional architecture as well as the company's cross-in-a-circle logo.

The design of the twin-domed Santa Fe depot at San Diego, California, dating from 1915, was a knowing translation of that

The station at Meriden, Connecticut was built in 1942 by the New York, New Haven & Hartford Railroad in a colonial revival style typical of New England. It replaced a late 19th-century Beaux Arts building, and was itself demolished in 1970.

of the early 19th-century mission San Luis Rey de Francia. Here, Renaissance, Moorish, and Spanish colonial architecture met the trains of the Santa Fe at the end of the Route of the Stars, the big names of Hollywood being loyal patrons of the railways. The station, which features the Santa Fe emblem in the tilework of its domed towers, was saved from demolition in 1972. Today, although you can still board a train here, one wing of the building houses the Museum of Contemporary Art San Diego.

Further north along the California coast, Los Angeles Union Station was completed in 1939 to designs by Donald Parkinson and Jan van der Linden. Its triumphant fusion of Art Deco, Spanish colonial, and Streamlined Moderne made it perhaps the last truly great US station in terms of design, and today a tourist destination as much as a busy railway terminus.

While the magnificent architecture of many US stations projected the romance of travel, the gritty freight yards that flanked them were a reminder that goods traffic was the backbone of US railroading. Crosstown freight trains could once be seen rumbling between docks and Manhattan skyscrapers or across quarters of Kansas City, New Orleans, and Los Angeles. New York's West 60th Street freight yard once occupied a huge site between 11th Avenue and the River Hudson. Purchased by Donald Trump in the 1970s, this prime real estate is now a luxury riverfront development.

Chicago, according to the poet Carl Sandburg, was "Proud to be Hog Butcher, Tool Maker, Stacker of Wheat, Player with Railroads and Freight Handler to the Nation." Created from former swampland by a consortium of nine railroads, its Union Stockyards had grown by their peak in the 1920s into a square mile of livestock pens, slaughterhouses, and sidings served by 15 miles of railway track, employing 40,000 workers and butchering some ten million animals a year. Ancillary businesses sprang up manufacturing soap, leather, glue, fertilizer, pharmaceuticals, perfume, shoe polish, wigs, and violin strings. Refrigerated boxcars, developed from the 1870s, rolled prepared meat across the nation until, after World War II, the industry decentralized.

The Union Stockyards closed in 1971, and the site is now a business park. Significantly, it was here that the Armour Corporation had built its mechanized slaughterhouse, at one time the world's largest factory. Henry Ford came to watch the production line in action before going on to mass produce his Model-T automobile, which was in many ways the nemesis of the US passenger train.

Freight yards themselves were mechanized. Railroads were keen to advertise the efficiency of their piggyback systems, whereby goods were carried in containers on flatbed railcars, and then transferred to trucks at the depot for the journey across town to join another line. Ian Logan recalls his experience of the country's mighty marshalling or hump yards, where huge numbers of enormous freight trains are assembled as if by sleight of hand before setting out to all points of the American compass and even far beyond.

"Somebody told me I should go to Kansas City. They were selling wheat to Russia, and the whole city was covered in freight cars, so I flew down there and got in touch with the Burlington Yards. They got a man to walk round with me with an electric stick, because there were wild dogs everywhere."

Ian was allowed into the control tower to view the operation of the yard. "It's called a hump yard because there's a hump in the middle, and on the other side the tracks fan out in all directions. They push a freight car up the hump and then pull a switch in the signal box to send it along the right track, and then it rolls down under its own momentum."

These freight yards continue to impress, not so much with their efficiency but by their sheer scale. No one witnessing an American freight yard in action could ever doubt that the US is a giant among nations with an eager appetite for food, goods, and fuel. Even today, boxcars that have made their way from city to city and one yard to another may still advertise the glory of passenger lines lost to history, if not to the imagination.

Architectural Logos

Railroads often built their logos into the physical fabric of stations, internally and externally. From the tower of Cheyenne Station, Union Pacific's shield once dominated the prairie town, the Santa Fe's cross-in-circle was rendered in stucco and glazed tiles, and the long-defunct Pennsy's keystone can still be seen throughout the Northeast. Northern Pacific's Yin and Yang symbol adorns the restored Livingston Depot, Montana, in colorful relief.

Station Design

From the second half of the 19th century, railroad companies sought to express their identity and aspirations through station architecture, often with soaring towers that formed prominent landmarks in a pre-skyscraper age. They chose from a range of historicist styles to suit regional preferences. On the East Coast, Neoclassicism predominated, while Neo-Romanesque castles and cathedrals sprang up in many a Midwestern city. In the Southwest, the Santa Fe and other railroads paid tribute to the region's heritage with a series of beautiful stations in the Spanish Mission style.

The Neo-Romanesque Union Station in Montgomery, Alabama was built by the local architect Benjamin Bosworth Smith for the Louisville & Nashville Railroad in 1898. The length of its façade was a result of the "Jim Crow" laws requiring racially segregated facilities. Since the building's restoration as a visitor center, the beige paint that covered it when Ian Logan took this photo in the 1970s has been removed to reveal the original red brickwork and limestone facings. The 600-foot cast-iron trainshed just visible at either side was considered a triumph of engineering at the time of its construction.

Left: Daniel Burnham's Union Station, seen here in 1974, was designed to match the Neoclassical dignity of the federal government buildings, museums, and galleries that flank the National Mall in Washington, DC.

Romanesque Revival

Inspired by Ruskin and William Morris, the American architect Henry Hobson Richardson (1838–86) developed and popularized a Neo-Romanesque idiom in buildings such the Trinity Church in Boston. After his early death, "Richardsonian Romanesque," as it came to be known, was carried west and south along the railroads by station architects, whose buildings continued to embody its medieval inspiration and ecclesiastical origins.

Opposite: With its lofty clock tower, turrets, and gables, Nashville's Union Station is one of the most imposing examples of Romanesque Revival railway architecture in the United States. Completed in 1900 to a design by Richard Montfort, the Louisville & Nashville Railroad's chief engineer, the depot closed to passengers in 1979; after almost a decade of dereliction, it was renovated for use as a hotel, and is listed in the National Register of Historic Places.

Above: Henry Van Brunt's Neo-Romanesque depot at Cheyenne, Wyoming was built in 1887 from sandstone quarried at Fort Collins, Colorado. "One would almost forget himself and think he was in the Crystal Palace of old, that formerly adorned the city of London," wrote the Cheyenne Sun's reporter on its opening, "while taking a stroll up and down its ample halls and corridors." Passenger services ceased in 1979 and, like many other historic US stations, Cheyenne is now a museum.

New Deal Deco

Built between 1929 and 1933, the year Franklin D. Roosevelt began his first term as President, Cincinnati Union Terminal was one of the last great railroad stations to be built in the United States. Train services ended in 1972 and, despite designation as a National Historic Landmark in 1977, the station fell into disrepair before reopening as the Cincinnati Museum Center in 1990. It was restored between 2016 and 2018.

Left and right: The Art Deco interiors of Cincinnati Union Terminal were the work of the industrial designer Paul Philippe Cret, while the mural mosaics, depicting the history of the city and the dignity of labor, were by the German-born artist Winold Reiss.

Spanish Mission Style

SOUTHERN PACIFIC TERMINUS, 3RD AND TOWNSEND, SAN FRANCISCO, CAL.

Conquered from Mexico in 1848, Arizona, Texas, New Mexico, and California boast a rich heritage of mission churches built by the Spanish in the 17th and 18th centuries. Among the oldest buildings in the United States, they combine European Baroque elements such as ornate doorways with local materials such as adobe (mud brick). The result is a distinctive regional architecture that provided a model for station builders keen to celebrate the culture of the Southwest.

Southern Pacific's depot on Third and Townsend in San Francisco was built in 1914 in the Spanish Mission style. Sadly, this splendid building was demolished in 1976.

Right: The Los Angeles architects John and Donald Parkinson brought Art Deco flair to the Spanish Mission style in the city's Union Station. Opened in 1939, it is still a functioning station.

The monumental waiting room of Los Angeles Union Station draws on the Classical Moderne idiom of the New Deal era. Its wall tiles and marble floor are based on the pattern of a Navajo blanket, while the seating is Art Deco. The 62-foot high timber-beamed ceiling pays tribute to the region's Spanish church architecture.

Built in 1915 by the San Francisco practice Bakewell & Brown, San Diego's Santa Fe Depot is perhaps the finest surviving example of Spanish Mission revival architecture. The zigzag tilework on the twin domes is embellished with the Santa Fe Railway's logo, which is also incorporated into the interior tiling. The building was saved from demolition in 1972 and restored.

Carrying the Message

Freight always made up a large part of US rail traffic, and every major city had yards for its distribution. Many were built with an incline or hump, so that cars could be pushed uphill by a switcher engine and then allowed to roll down the other side, where switches would send them onto the correct track. Since many railroads ran their own yards, cars would be interchanged from one to another.

Piggyback transfer was an early 20th-century innovation to speed up service and broaden market areas. This was a method of transportation in which trailers were lifted from flatcars and attached to trucks to be driven to or from the customer. For many years, railroad companies operated their own fleets of trucks for this purpose, prominently advertising their freight services on the trailers, which thus became moving billboards as they traveled.

Above: Built in a utilitarian modern style by the Chicago, Milwaukee, St. Paul & Pacific Railroad in 1917, the Freight House that adjoins the Union Station at Davenport, Iowa played an important role in the commercial development of this junction city on the Mississippi, providing a covered space for loading and unloading boxcars. Since its restoration in the 1990s, the Freight House has been home to bars, restaurants, a comedy club, and, most recently, a farmers' market.

Right: A boxcar leased by Pacific Fruit Express stands in New York's West 60th Street freight yard, which occupied a huge site along the Hudson riverfront from 59th to 72nd Street. The New York Times printing plant, just behind, was opened next to the yard in 1959 to secure rapid rail delivery. By 1975 the presses had become obsolete and the newspaper moved to New Jersey. The yard closed soon afterward, and the site has since become luxury housing.

Signwriters used every inch of space on freight trains to ram home their companies' messages. Apparently painted freehand, Western Pacific's trademark feather is here blown up to fill the entire side of a boxcar.
On a train of wagons at Manhattan's West 60th Street Yard *(right)*, the impact of Canadian National's bold, Modernist logo is amplified by repetition.

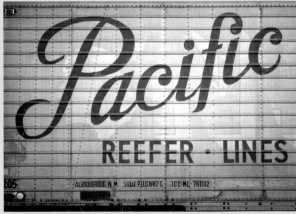

The logos of the Seaboard Air Line, Illinois Central, and Union Pacific adorn 1970s piggyback trailers and a reefer or refrigerator car propped up in freight yards, ready to be loaded onto flatcars or driven across town.

4. SELLING THE DREAM

Phoebe says

And Phoebe knows

That smoke and cinders

Spoil good clothes

Phoebe Snow was a fictional character created by Earnest Elmo Calkins of the New York advertising agency Calkins & Holden. Phoebe means pure or bright and, fresh-fallen, snow is white and light. Phoebe's job, from her public debut in 1900, was to ride the long-distance trains of the Delaware, Lackawanna & Western Railroad between New Jersey and Buffalo in a sequence of entertaining and hugely popular adverts commissioned by the Lackawanna Road.

By 1900 American express and Pullman trains could be very comfortable and well serviced. If there was a problem for passengers, especially if they happened to be well-dressed women, it was grime. Smoke and soot belching from the funnels of muscular, coal-fired locomotives meant a lot of laundry and, at worst, ruined outfits. This was down to a combination of low-grade coal and the still inefficient drafting and exhaust arrangements of steam locomotives. The incomplete combustion of coal resulted in the ejection of soot, cinders, and even lumps of blazing fuel across train roofs, through train windows, along platforms, across backyards and their hanging wash, and passing fields and rivers.

In terms of fuel, the Lackawanna had an ace up its sleeve. Its main line passed through the anthracite belts of Pennsylvania. With its high carbon content, anthracite is the most efficient and cleanest burning form of coal. Enter Phoebe Snow, a vision in the latest white fashions, either seated in a spotless restaurant car decorated with fresh roses:

A cosy seat

A dainty treat

Make Phoebe's

Happiness complete

With linen white

And silver bright

Upon the road

Of anthracite

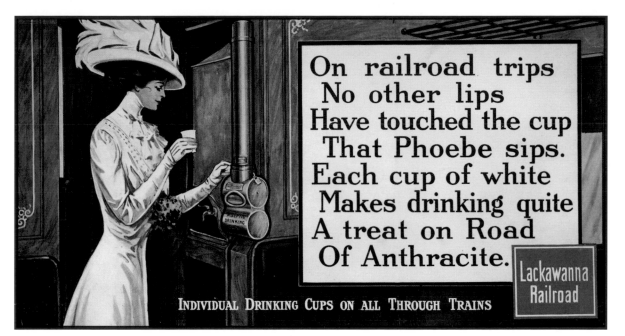

On railroad trips
No other lips
Have touched the cup
That Phoebe sips.
Each cup of white
Makes drinking quite
A treat on Road
Of Anthracite.

Lackawanna Railroad

INDIVIDUAL DRINKING CUPS ON ALL THROUGH TRAINS

Or leaning from the balcony of a Pullman car admiring the passing scenery:

My gown stays white

From morn till night

Upon the road

Of anthracite

Her features drawn from those of the model Marion Murray, Phoebe Snow did much to popularize the Lackawanna. She was also the first fictional character used to tell stories in US advertising. More than this, her railway adventures on posters, billboards, calendars, and postcards were key to the development of the radical new concepts that Calkins called the "soft sell" and "consumer engineering."

Picking up from Calkins's cue, the Chesapeake & Ohio Railroad introduced the traveling public to Chessie the Cat. Chessie, an adorable kitten tucked up asleep in a berth of an overnight C&O train, first appeared in the September 1933 issue of *Fortune*. "Sleep Like a Kitten and Arrive as Fresh as a Daisy in Air-Conditioned Comfort," purred the C&O ad. The ensuing campaign worked like a dream, with Chessie's cuteness and fame stretching across the country. She was America's Sleepheart, a comforting image in an era of high unemployment and destitution. Like Chessie, Americans needed to dream.

Chessie's origins were wrapped in myth and fable. One story doing the rounds in the early Thirties was that she was a real-life abandoned kitten rescued by a C&O train crew who named her after the railroad. Chessie was, in fact, an etching in a newspaper by

Guido Gruenewald, a Viennese artist, that caught the eye of L. C. Probert, the C&O's public relations and advertising manager. Probert paid $5 for the right to use Gruenewald's kitten. His in-house ad department got to work and Chessie became an instant draw and overnight success.

Peake, a tomcat mate, joined Chessie alongside kittens Nip and Tuck. Calendars followed, distributed in tens of thousands along with jewelry, plates, playing cards, musical boxes, and two books by Ruth Caroll, Chessie and Chessie and Her Kittens. In a wartime advert, Chessie is seen asleep above an image of one of the C&O's brand new H8 Class 2-6-6-6 locomotives at the head of the George Washington express. Thunderous mobile power plants, the H8s were among the most powerful steam locomotives ever built. At full throttle, their exhausts might have woken the devil, but not Chessie.

Given the success of the kitten campaign, unsurprisingly the C&O chose to call itself the Chessie Route. Chessie remained part of C&O advertising campaigns until 1971 when Amtrak took over the railroad's passenger services. Reworked as a stylized graphic logo, Chessie appeared anew on the flanks of freight boxcars of the Chessie System, an amalgamation of the C&O, Baltimore & Ohio, and Western Maryland railways.

This nicknaming of routes was hugely popular among US railroads. The Central of Georgia was the Route of the Nancy Hanks, an express train named after an undefeated racehorse. The Missouri Pacific was the Route of the Eagles after its Delta Eagle, Valley Eagle, Colorado Eagle, and Aztec Eagle expresses. The Mount Tamalpais & Muir Woods Railway called itself The Crookedest Railroad in the World. This was a reference to the mountainous Californian railway's twisting track – 281 curves in just over eight miles – and not to the financial culture of its management.

The most improbable nickname was surely the Northern Pacific's curious culinary appellation, Route of the Great Big Baked Potato. The line passed through Washington State's Yakima Valley, where

The enormous spuds grown in Washington state proved a hit in the Northern Pacific's dining cars, and became a prominent selling point in the railroad's advertising.

The enormous spuds grown in Washington state proved a hit in the Northern Pacific's dining cars, and became a prominent selling point in the railroad's advertising.

giant potatoes flourished. When slow baked, as the Northern Pacific's dining car superintendent Hazen Titus discovered in 1908, these slow-selling giant root vegetables proved to be delicious. Promoted heavily, they were an instant success. The NP's Seattle food warehouse featured a forty-foot long Great Big Baked Potato on its roof. Electric lights caused the butter served with it to glow and its eyes to wink. One verse from a song concocted by the railroad went:

> 'Twas laying on a platter
> Sure something just immense
> Served with a spoon and butter
> And it only cost ten cents.

Otherwise, the Northern Pacific was known as the Main Street of the North West, which sounds more dignified, if less fun. Unabashed, the Denver & Rio Grande sold itself as the Scenic Line of the World. No one would doubt the Union Pacific's boast

We Can Handle It, although some might have wondered about the very name of the Frisco. This was the St. Louis-San Francisco, a railway that served nine Midwestern and Southern states for over a century, yet never got anywhere near San Francisco either geographically or politically: it was the last line to put an end to Jim Crow laws by which black and white passengers were separated in station waiting rooms and rest rooms, and on board trains. The Katy Line which, for a number of years, hosted a logo in the guise of what looked like a teenage girl's signature was in fact the MKT – The Missouri-Kansas-Texas Railway. Later it was abbreviated to KT, and thus Katy.

The majestic landscapes of the West featured prominently in Santa Fe Railroad advertising such as this 1949 poster by Don Perceval, tempting hikers to visit Yosemite National Park in California by train.

Some railroads with scenic routes heading south and west across deserts and mountains turned advertising into not just a fine art, but art itself. In 1912 the Santa Fe commissioned Thomas Moran to paint the Grand Canyon as part of its promotion of a thrilling landscape to which it could convey its passengers. The western railroads played key roles in the creation of US National Parks – Yellowstone, Yosemite, Glacier, and Grand Canyon – guessing, rightly, that these sublime landscapes would appeal to Americans looking out from the windows of city blocks and commuter trains and dreaming of wild open spaces.

When in 1898 the Southern Pacific sponsored *Sunset* magazine to promote rail tourism, it commissioned artists to evoke the spirit of the landscapes its trains steamed through in the belief that paintings were able to heighten a sense of mystery and fantasy as yet unobtainable through photography. In the 1920s, Maurice Logan painted instantly memorable and lyrically haunting scenes of pueblos, dude ranches, and, especially, Native Americans, who were seen as a kind of lost civilization. Passengers might as well be traveling by flying carpet in some *One Thousand and One Nights* fantasy as in air-conditioned cars drawn by reciprocating steam engines.

Inspired by new European art and the highly imaginative posters commissioned from artists by Frank Pick, managing director of the London Underground, the company gave Logan free rein to paint what he saw and knew would appeal to large audiences – a girl on a California beach, a young woman riding a horse with a Yosemite peak behind her, the balcony tail car of a Southern Pacific train disappearing into the cleft of the Carrizo Gorge, a valley in the Jacumba Mountains in San Diego County, California.

Between 1929 and 1932, the Great Depression reduced passenger traffic on the railways by half while the use of automobiles remained steady. The railways had a mighty job on their hands to encourage passengers back on to their trains. Just as in the Hollywood film industry, the notion of escape was all important.

The Santa Fe made great play of the Native American heritage of its route through the Southwest. The exterior of the 1937 *Super Chief* was the work of the mellifluously named Leland Knickerbocker,

Gulf, Mobile & Ohio

GM&O

FOUR TRAINS DAILY In Each Direction Chicago-St. Louis
Including ONLY OVERNITE SERVICE BETWEEN CHICAGO-ST. LOUIS

Left: A 1962 timetable sports the famous winged logo adopted after the Gulf, Mobile & Northern merged with the Mobile & Ohio in 1940.

Right: A Union Pacific locomotive appears to charge toward the viewer from this Los Angeles billboard.

a color stylist with General Motors' Electro-Motive Division. Knickerbocker called his paint scheme the Warbonnet. The bright red front of the GM diesels was adorned and wrapped around with a yellow winged Native American emblem described as an "Indian head with trailing feathers of a warbonnet." However described, it was a stunning design. The interiors of the stainless-steel Pullman cars were fitted out by the designer Sterling McDonald in a palette of subtle colors embellished with Native American motifs. The artist Hernando Villa's stylized portraits of chieftains in full-feathered headdresses featured on timetables, posters, and dining-car menus perused by people who were highly unlikely to see any American looking like this outside the walls of some new Art Deco picture house or a Wild West show playing in town.

"Getting there is half the fun," claimed the cruise line Cunard, and it was a motto all railroads with an eye to the future did well to heed during the 1930s. PR departments raised their game, using every device in the design toolbox to bring style to dining cars, sleepers, catering, uniforms, advertising, and all the chic accoutrements of modern train travel, from monogrammed napkins and cocktail glasses to matchboxes and ashtrays.

Another approach was to pretend all was well. From the early 1930s, the New York Central commissioned Leslie Ragan to paint stirring cityscapes, industrial landscapes, and powerful steam trains thundering along its Hudson River racetrack as if the Great Depression had never happened. Energetic marketing and advertising, whether through the agency of sleeping kittens, giant potatoes, corporate competence, or fantasy, might have been a cover for the state of the railways as passenger numbers fell, but it could also pivot towards the future and was at the heart of the railroad's next alluring gamble: streamlining. Could the arts of advertising, styling, and design rescue the American passenger train and even raise it to new heights of speed and comfort?

GET A GOOD THING
GOING, SHIP IT...
6900
6900
UNION PACIFIC
6900
UNION

The Soft Sell

Railway executives and staff were endlessly inventive when it came to projecting a distinctive image, using landmarks, personalities, and even cuddly animals as emblems. Quick to grasp the promotional value of the nicknames given to them by the public, they were seldom too proud or pompous to adopt them. The Chesapeake & Ohio abbreviated itself to Chessie, the name of its kitten mascot. The Missouri-Kansas-Texas Railway morphed into Katy, while the St. Louis-San Francisco Railway was happy to be known as the Frisco. Its slogan Ship It On the Frisco was but one of many snappy catchlines thought up by railroad wordsmiths; Be Specific – Ship Union Pacific was another memorable example.

Missouri Pacific's bold red buzzsaw logo stamped a uniform brand identity on a range of media, from timetables to matchbooks.

Proud of the fact that all its trains ran to Washington, DC, the Baltimore & Ohio Railroad made the dome of the US Capitol the centerpiece of its branding. The building also featured on the ornate cover of the monthly magazine the company produced from 1897 to 1911 for passengers on its flagship Royal Blue line *(left)*.

Her elegant costumes unbesmirched by soot from the Lackawanna's anthracite-powered trains, Phoebe Snow was massively popular for more than a decade, appearing in comic-strip graphics and dreamy photoshoots from the early 1900s.

Miss Snow may scan
Through journey's span
Each keen and faithful
Tower-man,
Whose levers bright
Are swung aright
Upon the Road
of Anthracite.

Lackawanna
Railroad

Lackawanna

THE ROUTE OF PHOEBE SNOW

Brief History of the Railroad with Photographs and Description of its Motive Power

Lackawanna Railroad

The Return of Phoebe Snow

Back at the turn of the century, when railroad travel was "in plush," although less refined than the service of to-day, an auburn-haired maiden, garbed in immaculate white and adorned by a dainty corsage of violets, made her bow on the American scene.

Her name was Phoebe Snow. And her sparkling-white dress and hat symbolized cleanliness of travel on the Lackawanna Railroad. The Lackawanna of those days was one of the few railroads whose locomotives took the "sin" out of cinders by burning hard coal instead of soft coal.

Penrhyn Stanlaws and other celebrated portrait artists glorified Miss Phoebe Snow with palette and canvas. Vaudeville vocalists sang her praises. Poets and wags, too, contributed to Phoebe Snow's popularity. Advertisements, set to rhyme and illustrated with action pictures of Miss Phoebe, appeared in profusion in street-cars, in magazines and in newspapers.

Typical of these verses was the one in which Phoebe admitted:

*"I won my fame and wide acclaim
For Lackawanna's splendid name
By keeping bright and snowy white
Upon the Road of Anthracite."*

But when Phoebe Snow had reached her peak of popularity someone started a war — the first of the two World Wars. Then the Government took over the railroads, which were ordered to burn soft coal. That order restored the forgotten cinders and grime of Lackawanna travel. Phoebe Snow and her garb of dainty white disappeared from the scene for 27 long years.

It was not until 1944, during the second World War, that Phoebe Snow was "reincarnated" by the Lackawanna. She reappeared in Lackawanna advertisements, reeling off jingles as in the old days. This time Miss Phoebe extolled the Grade A job her railroad was doing in the war effort. Gone were the debonair white hat and gown, also the pert bouquet of violets. The new Phoebe Snow — lovelier than ever — made her wartime debut bedecked in natty service uniform and jaunty overseas cap.

Today, new equipment bears the legend, "Lackawanna — the Route of Phoebe Snow." And like "Granny," an ultra-modern Phoebe Snow in glorified white uniform, soon will break forth in verse again to tell the story of Lackawanna's new super-speed Diesel locomotives and of its streamlined, air-conditioned trains which will provide clean, smooth-riding, speedy and *safe* travel.

PHOEBE SNOW — TODAY

THE ROUTE OF *Phoebe Snow*

TIME TABLES

APRIL 28, 1957

Time Shown in this folder is DAYLIGHT SAVING TIME except as otherwise shown on Page 3.

Form 10

Pensioned off when anthracite was reserved for warships during World War I, Phoebe Snow was revived some 27 years later, clad in a crisp white service uniform. From 1949 to 1966 the Lackawanna ran a popular express train called the *Phoebe Snow* from Hoboken, New Jersey to Chicago via Buffalo.

THE ROUTE OF PHOEBE SNOW

Lackawanna

Nicknames

One of the most successful and longest-lived railroad nicknames was Chessie, derived from the cute kitten mascot adopted by the Chesapeake & Ohio. After its amalgamation with the Western Maryland and the Baltimore & Ohio in 1972, Chessie lived on, incorporated into the name of the holding company, the Chessie System, and painted in a simplified, stylized form on the sides of locomotives and other rolling stock.

CHESAPEAKE AND OHIO LINES

Sleep like a Kitten

ROUTE OF
THE GEORGE WASHINGTON
THE SPORTSMAN
THE F.F.V.

MAY 16, 1943

TIME TABLES

Chessie led the Chesapeake & Ohio's 1930s advertising *(opposite)* and was instantly recognizable in the stripped-down graphics of the 1970s.

The Missouri-Kansas-Texas Railway's reporting mark MKT was soon abbreviated to KT, pronounced Katy. Taken up by the company, the nickname appeared on freight cars *(right)*, on matchbooks and on postcards announcing the inaugural run of the streamlined *Texas Special* in 1948 *(left)*.

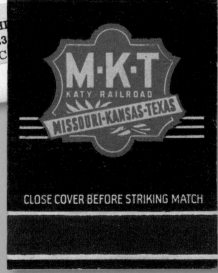

Slogans

Railroads were early adopters of slogans, excelling in short forms that could be incorporated into their logos. All were designed to convey a clear message quickly and memorably. Exploiting rolling stock as free billboards, many companies splashed their slogans in large letters across the sides of boxcars.

Union Pacific's slogans, photographed by Ian Logan in Los Angeles in the 1970s, ranged from famous catchlines to safety warnings. True to the company ethos, they credited the staff members who had dreamed them up. Engineers drove over the tag-line Dependable Transportation painted in capitals beneath their cab windows.

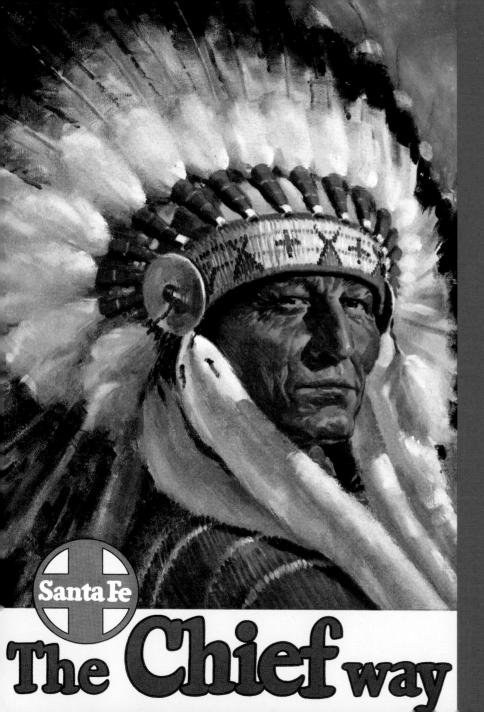

Santa Fe

The Chief way

Native American Imagery

The Atchison, Topeka & Santa Fe Railway's use of Native American imagery in its promotional material dates back to the late 19th century. Its catering arm, run by the English hotelier Fred Harvey, employed a German immigrant called Herman Schweizer to collect Navajo, Hopi, and Apache textiles and ceramics, which it displayed in a museum set up in 1902 at its flagship hotel in Albuquerque. Soon, these artifacts were featured in the railroad's calendars and became a staple of its advertising. In the 1920s, the company even launched a series of Indian Detours – chauffeur-driven excursions in "Harveycars" to the pueblos of New Mexico.

Once the Santa Fe called its luxury Chicago to Los Angeles service the *Chief* in 1926, the Native American theme became embodied in the names of the trains. A decade later, the *Chief* was joined by the even more state-of-the-art, diesel-powered *Super Chief*, and the fleet subsequently expanded to include the *Texas Chief* and finally, in 1954, the *San Francisco Chief*.

Not everyone was impressed by this wholesale commodification of Native American culture. "The Southwest is the great playground of the white American," wrote D. H. Lawrence in 1924. "And the Indian, with his long hair and bits of pottery and blankets… he's a wonderful live toy to play with."

Opposite: Based on a painting by Hernando Villa, this 1947 poster invokes the romance of the West with a chief resplendent in his warbonnet.

Right: The Santa Fe relaunched its Native American advertising at the start of the 1930s with its dependable Chief logo woven into its insignia.

Texas
Chief

SANTA FE

Santa Fe

Daily Pullman-Chair Car Streamliner
between the Great Lakes
and the Texas Gulf Coast

Santa Fe

the
Chief
is still chief

fastest train
via any line to
Southern
California

Extra fast, Extra fine, Extra fare

Far left: A 1955 brochure for the *Texas Chief* features its dramatic Warbonnet livery beneath the Native American headdress it was designed to echo.

Left: The Santa Fe Native American chief is given a modish Art Deco styling on a 1920s timetable cover.

Right: The rugged grandeur of the Southwest featured prominently in Santa Fe promotions; in this 1954 magazine advertisement, the *San Francisco Chief* streaks past Temple Rock, New Mexico.

Overleaf: An embossed aluminum plaque combining the Santa Fe logo with the profile of a Native American chief, headdress streaming in the wind, was affixed to the side of the railroad's passenger cars and locomotives.

San Francisco Chief

Santa Fe

Santa Fe

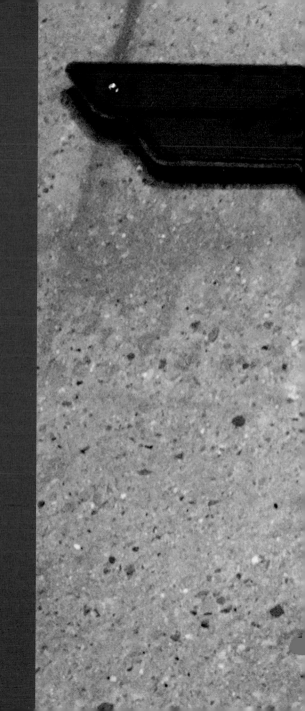

Logo Evolution
Union Pacific

The original Union Pacific emblem, a mountain elk, made way for decorative typographic logos before the company arrived at its famous shield in 1886. Wanting an image that conveyed the railroad's patriotic origins, the company's Vice President T. J. Potter asked the passenger agent Edward L. Lomax to create a new look. Lomax came up with a design based on a special agent's badge. The Stars and Stripes coloring was added in 1888, and the shield took on its present form in 1949, when the railroad's President E. Roland Harriman replaced the curvilinear lettering with a crisp Modernist font.

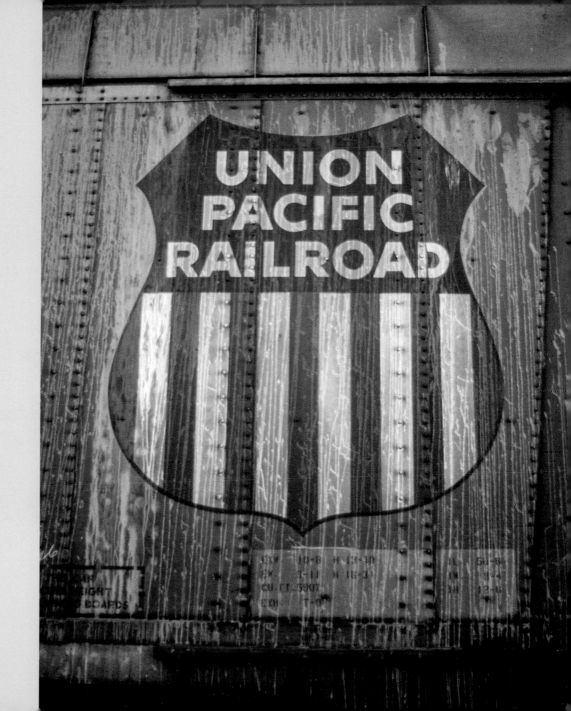

Steam locomotives sported the Union Pacific badge in front of their smokeboxes, as on this Big Boy photographed by Ian Logan in the 1970s. Boxcars received the full stars-and-stripes treatment *(right).*

New York Central and Pennsylvania Railroads

The New York Central Railroad's distinctive oval was reportedly suggested by an employee in 1904, and underwent a number of changes in the course of the 20th century. In 1935, the "Lines" legend, reversed out of a black background, was replaced by one reading "System," and in 1955 the lettering was changed to a simpler sans-serif font. The stylish herald with "Central" in cursive script over a series of rules was applied to refrigerator cars from 1956. The famous cigar band herald was adopted at a 1959 shareholders' meeting.

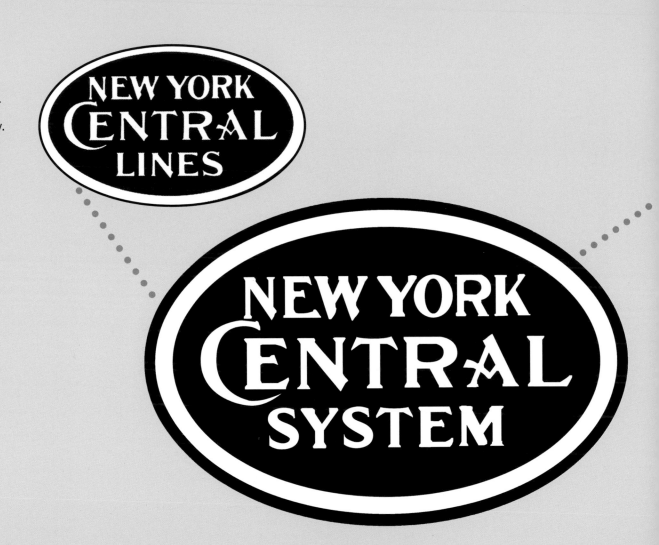

The Pennsylvania Railroad herald was modeled
on a keystone, a symbol of the Commonwealth of
Pennsylvania. In use from the late 19th century, it
became one of the best known corporate symbols in
the United States, and underwent little change until
the ornate lettering was replaced by a plainer sans-
serif font in the 1950s. Both the NYC's cigar band and
the Pennsylvania keystone disappeared in 1968, when
the two railroads amalgamated to form Penn Central.
The new company's modern logo, with its intertwined
P and C, was known to railfans as the "mating worms."

American Financial Enterprises, Inc.

BORDER AREA TO BE TOLU

EDGING TO BE BUFF

BACKGROUND AREA TO BE TOLUIDINE RED, P.R.R. SHADE

MONOGRAM TO BE BUFF, P.R.R. SHADE REF. 47-2616

2'-1½"

21"

17⅛"

2¼"

1¹⁵⁄₁₆"

4'

BLACK ENAMEL

SHADOW AREA TO BE BLACK ENAMEL, P.R.R. REF. 47-2218

American Financial Enterprises, Inc.

PENN CENTRAL

The On-Board Experience

Railroads stamped their insignia onto every aspect of on-board service, including menu cards, tableware, coasters, placemats, and even smokers' accessories. Great attention was paid to dining cars and their accoutrements. As early as 1898, the *Locomotive Engineer* of New York reported that "The dining car service on the trains of the Nickel Plate road is something that strikes the traveler as approaching perfection," while the Santa Fe boasted that "It's almost worth taking a trip just to eat a Fred Harvey meal." No opportunity was missed to ensure that passengers' comfort and convenience were indelibly associated with the brand.

Opposite: The cover of an early 20th-century Nickel Plate Road menu extends the promise of fine dining; from the range of Club Suppers listed inside, passengers could choose a one-dollar meal of little-neck clams, tenderloin steak, and strawberries and cream. The wine list included Haut Sauternes, St. Julien claret, and champagne from Veuve Clicquot, Mumm, and Moët et Chandon.

Right: In a late 1940s advertisement in the Saturday Evening Post, two cowboys gaze in wonder at the elegant meal being served aboard a Santa Fe Railway dining car.

"Gee, that's Eatin'"

This young man knows a good thing when he sees it.

The cheerful dining-car accessories of the 1960s and 1970s took branding to the table top. A Union Pacific coaster tempts passengers with a cocktail, the Great Northern's mountain goat is pressed into service as a waiter, while a Spokane, Portland & Seattle diesel speeds across one of the railway's placemats.

In the heyday of US passenger rail transport, smoking was not an offense but a promotional opportunity. The St. Louis-San Francisco Railway offered branded matchbooks to smokers, while the Canadian Pacific provided metal ashtrays embossed with their beaver emblem.

5.STREAMLINE STYLE

May 26th, 1934. Shortly after 7 a.m. Central Daylight Time, the Chicago, Burlington & Quincy Railroad's *Zephyr* purred away from Denver, Colorado on a dawn-to-dusk sprint to Chicago, 1,015 miles to the east. Nothing like this gleaming, lightweight, polished stainless-steel, diesel-electric train had been seen before. Dubbed the *Silver Streak*, the futuristic streamliner, its wheels all but invisible, flashed across manned rural crossings and rocketed past passenger and freight trains held in loops and sidings for this vision of the future to pass.

Cruising where possible at 100 m.p.h. and topping 112½ m.p.h., the *Zephyr* arrived in Chicago in thirteen hours and five minutes, two and a half hours early, having maintained an average speed of more than 77 m.p.h. A regular heavyweight steam express took twenty-five hours to make the same trip. Cinema newsreels, radio stations, and the front pages of newspapers across the United States covered the story.

Once in Chicago, the three-coach train was dispatched to the city's hugely popular Century of Progress exhibition before setting off on a tour of 222 cities across thirty-one states. President Franklin Roosevelt was one of the two million Americans who came to see it . Zephyr mania saw the name applied to automobiles, musical instruments, and football teams. That December, cinemas screened *The Silver Streak*, a melodramatic RKO feature advertised as a "streamline saga" starring the Burlington train.

The Pioneer *Zephyr* was not the first streamlined diesel train to be built in the US. That accolade belonged to the Union Pacific's *M-10000*. Designed by UP's energetic chief engineer Otto Jabelmann and named the *City of Salina*, this Buck Rogers-style lightweight Pullman was unveiled nearly a year before the *Zephyr*, but was then sent on a publicity tour and did not go into passenger service until after the launch of the *Zephyr*, running between Kansas City, Missouri, and Salina, Kansas. It never made it to Hollywood; not only did *M-10000* lack the visual appeal of the Burlington train, but Union Pacific had turned down RKO's request to use the train in the film that, with an altogether more glamorous mechanical star, became *The Silver Streak*.

Opposite: Raymond Loewy's 1936 sketch shows how the Pennsylvania Railroad's existing K4s engines would look under a streamline shroud. Like the New York Central, the Pennsy preferred a cosmetic lift to a total rebuild.

Left: Billed by Union Pacific as "modern art," the M-10000 was the first streamlined passenger train to be built in the United States, although the Burlington *Zephyr* would go into regular service before it.

The Burlington's popular, wind-cheating *Zephyr* proved to be far more than a passing sensation. Ten years down the line, it had clocked 1,676,000 miles in service and spawned sibling streamliners, notably the *Twin Cities Zephyrs* that revolutionized the Burlington's route from Chicago to Minneapolis-St. Paul.

Streamlining was a timely and compelling response to the financial threat facing not just the railroads but the entire US economy as the Great Depression followed grimly in the wake of the 1929 Wall Street Crash. Despite high unemployment and widespread poverty, car ownership was on the increase, and railroads were losing both passenger and freight traffic. What might revive railway finances was a cinematic flourish of some sort. Combining aerodynamics with Art Deco and Moderne styling, streamlining offered both the image and the reality of speed, fuel efficiency, and cleanliness.

The technical inspiration came originally from Germany. A superbly engineered two-car diesel-electric streamliner, the *Fliegender Hamburger,* had made its debut in May 1933, shortly after Adolf Hitler was appointed Chancellor. The beautifully turned out, cream and violet Deutsche Reichsbahn express sprinted the 178 miles between Berlin and Hamburg in 138 minutes, reeling in mile after mile at a steady 100 m.p.h. The British responded with a new generation of streamlined Art Deco steam expresses, notably the London & North Eastern Railway's *Silver Jubilee* and *Coronation*. In July 1938, one of the streamlined A4 Pacific locomotives designed for these services, 4468 *Mallard*, took, and still holds, the world speed record of 126 m.p.h. for steam traction.

A Baltimore & Ohio herald from the late 1940s depicts its streamlined steam express the *Cincinnatian* speeding alongside one of its E-series diesels.

LINKING 13 GREAT STATES WITH THE NATION

B&O

What these German, British, and American trains had in common, whether steam or diesel, was a fresh look that manifested itself in bright new color schemes, the latest in exterior styling and interior design, up-to-the-minute graphics, badges, and logos, underpinned by decidedly modern advertising and marketing campaigns that helped sear their image into the popular imagination.

The Burlington *Zephyrs* were the product of the research and imaginative skills of the aeronautical engineer Albert Dean, the advanced welding techniques of Edward Budd, the design flair of architects Paul Philippe Cret and John Harbeson, and the vision of Burlington's dynamic president, Ralph Budd. Wanting his streamliners to be the last word in contemporary railroad design, he decided their name had to begin with Z. By chance, Budd had been reading the *Canterbury Tales*. In the Prologue, Chaucer writes, "When Zephyr also has, with his sweet breath, Quickened again . . ." The reference to the god of the west wind settled the matter. Racing with or against the west wind, the first two Burlington streamliners were known as the *Train of the Gods* and the *Train of the Goddesses*. Their passenger cars were named after the Roman deities Apollo, Jupiter, Mars, Ceres, Diana, and Venus, evoking notions of beauty, power, authority, and speed.

Until General Motors' Electro-Motive Division got into its stride in the late 1930s, however, diesel could not produce anything approaching the horsepower of a big steam engine, restricting the number of cars that could be pulled and the on-board facilities provided. So the new streamline style was applied to the older technology, and it was a generation of mighty steam locomotives, modeled on sleek, wind-cheating lines, that powered the most glamorous streamliners. These included the Pennsylvania's *Broadway Limited*, the *Hiawathas* of the Milwaukee Road, and the Southern Pacific's Coast *Daylight*.

THE CENTURY IN THE HIGHLANDS OF THE HUDSON

NEW YORK CENTRAL SYSTEM

The New York Central's powerful Class J3a Hudson steam locomotive was re-styled in 1938 with an Art Deco nose-case by Henry Dreyfuss.

The brightest star of all was surely the 1938 edition of the New York Central's *20th Century Limited*. A seamless fusion of the highest-quality engineering, design, and styling, this lengthy and magnificently equipped two-tone grey streamliner was "cleanlined" by the celebrated industrial artist Henry Dreyfuss, from the striking Trojan Helmet nose cone of Paul Kiefer's imperious Class J3a Hudson steam locomotives to every last detail of the cars. Lettering, logo, livery. Cutlery, napery, crockery. Cocktail glasses, matchboxes, concealed lighting, and refined modern décor. In terms of design, no train has bettered this mile-a-minute overnight New York–Chicago express.

The Dreyfuss-Kiefer *20th Century Limited* was a work of art as well as a paragon of engineering and design. In 1940, *Fortune* magazine published Charles Sheeler's thrilling Precisionist painting *Rolling Power,* which focused, in photographic detail, on the driving wheels, piston rods, cranks, and levers of a J3a Hudson locomotive. It evoked to perfection the purposeful, powerful spirit of streamlined American steam.

Such was the visual impact of the mighty J3a Hudson that in 1939 *Fortune* magazine commissioned this oil painting of its driving wheels and piston rods, entitled *Rolling Power*, by the artist Charles Sheeler.

The painting is in the collection of the Smith College Museum of Art and is reproduced by courtesy of the Museum with the following accession details: SC 1940.18, Charles Sheeler, Rolling Power, 1939, oil on canvas, 22 ⅝ x 37 ⅝ in. Purchased with the Drayton Hillyer Fund, Smith College Museum of Art, Northampton, Massachusetts.

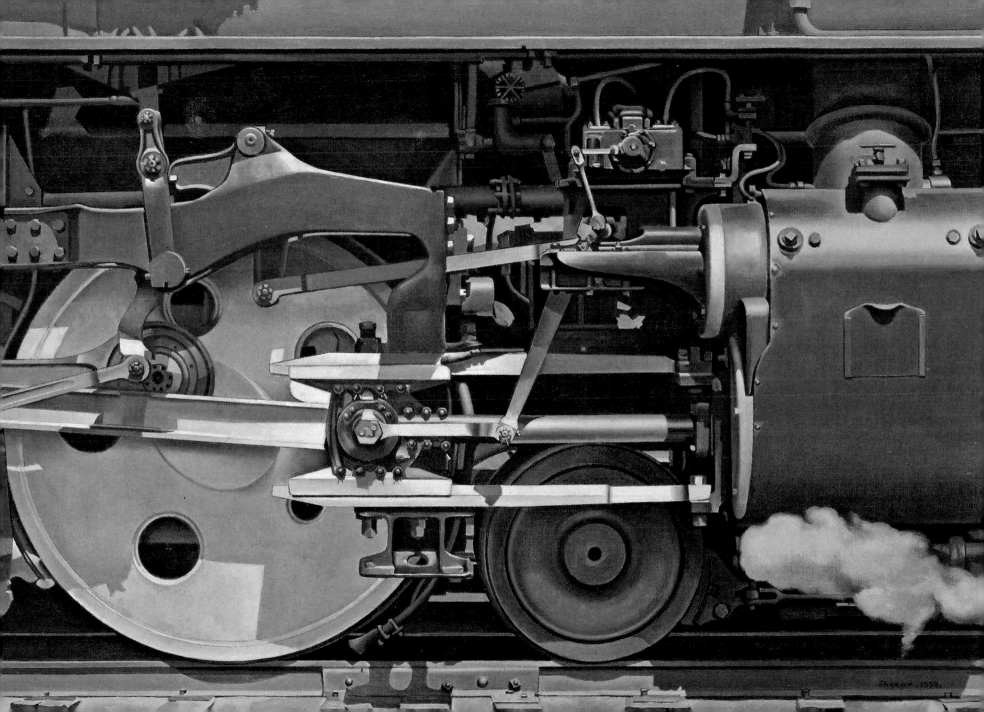

Railroads used every promotional means at their disposal, from matchbooks to magazine advertisements, to inform the public that they had streamlined long-established services. The *Meteor* and *Texas Special*, operated jointly by MKT and the St. Louis-San Francisco, and the Southern Pacific's *Golden State (right)* were re-equipped with EMD E7 diesel locomotives in 1947 and 1948.

For sheer speed, however, no streamliner could compare to the Milwaukee Road's *Hiawathas*, "speedlined" in 1938 by the German-American industrial artist Otto Kuhler. Passengers in the portholed Tip-Top-Tap cocktail bar could watch the Midwest racing by at 125 m.p.h. on a run that included the fastest point-to-point section ever timetabled for steam traction.

When streamliners reappeared after World War II in a blaze of new colors, décor, and graphic identities, diesel had all but replaced steam and a post-war generation of passenger cars offered a new take on long-distance travel. Extensively glazed observation carriages – like the Skytop Lounge cars designed by Brooks Stevens that were added to the *Hiawathas* in 1948, and the Burlington's Vista Domes – allowed passengers to ride as if on the roofs of carriages and enjoy unimpeded views of the epic American landscape. Uniformed stewardesses were hired,

most famously the Zephyrettes of the Burlington. These were the brainchild of the Burlington's Supervisor of Passenger Train Services, former schoolteacher and department store manager "Mama" Velma McPeek.

But for all the sophistication and style of trains like the *20th Century Limited*, business executives were turning to airlines for inter-city travel. With an increasing reliance on tourist traffic, dining cars might be replaced by meals from vending machines. As the Fifties gave way to the Sixties and Seventies, standards slipped further and custom fell away. There were honorable exceptions, none more so than the Santa Fe's *Super Chief*. This Chicago-to-California express had been the Train of the Stars from its launch in 1936. Re-equipped with General Motors diesel-electric locomotives and stainless-steel passenger cars the following year, it maintained much of its glamor and impeccable service up until

1971, when it was swallowed by Amtrak. From 1951, its passenger coaches included Pleasure Dome lounge cars and the following year, the *Super Chief* featured in the Gloria Swanson comedy *3 for Bedroom C.*

In their own ways, trains like Seaboard Air Line Railroad's green, yellow, and stainless-steel *Silver Meteor*, the rival Florida East Coast's blood-orange and yellow *Champion*, and the bright red and corrugated-aluminum *Texas Special* operated by the Katy and Frisco lines from St. Louis to San Antonio were memorable and stylish, yet in the end none of the great streamliners was able to hold the plane and the automobile at bay. Nor were such science-fiction-style odysseys as General Motors' *Aerotrain*, a curious low-slung lightweight train of 1955, its forty-seat cars running on pairs of air-suspended axles rather than conventional four-wheel bogies. These rode behind a diesel locomotive that, part aircraft, part automobile, was styled by GM's 28-year-old Chuck Jordan, who later took charge of the design of the exuberantly finned 1959 Cadillacs. The hard-riding *Aerotrain* was not a success, although one continued in service on Rock Island's commuter line from Chicago to Joliet into the 1960s.

Ways in which the streamlining bug infected American trains were, though, never less than fascinating. In 1940, the Western Maryland, storming through glorious Appalachian country and largely abandoned just thirty years later, applied a stirring Fireball herald to the locomotives and boxcars of its Western Maryland Fast Freight Line service, as if heavy US freight trains might just be streamliners, too. But then the design improvements to the Challenger 4-6-6-4 steam locomotives brought in to run these fast freights were the work of Otto Jabelmann, who had done so much to bring the first streamliner, the *M-10000*, to mechanical life.

D. C. 48—F. E. C. Streamliner
"The Champion"
at Miami, Florida

THE CHAMPION

FLORIDA EAST COAST
Railway

TIME TABLES

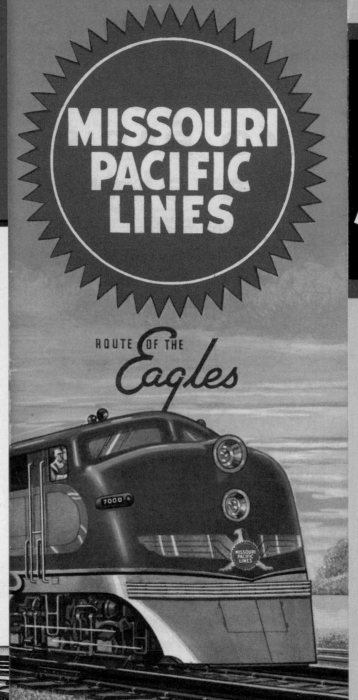

MISSOURI PACIFIC LINES

ROUTE OF THE
Eagles

THE MILWAUKEE ROAD

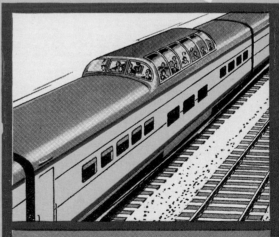

WESTERN "CITIES"
Streamliners

CITY OF SAN FRANCISCO • CITY OF PORTLAND
CITY OF LOS ANGELES • CITY OF DENVER
THE CHALLENGER

THE MILWAUKEE ROAD

SUPER DOME
Hiawathas

CHICAGO · MILWAUKEE · ST. PAUL
MINNEAPOLIS · MILES CITY · BUTTE
SPOKANE · SEATTLE · TACOMA

MISSOURI PACIFIC LINES

Issued August 13, 1944

Scenic Route . .
CALIFORNIA

ROYAL GORGE or MOFFAT TUNNEL
FEATHER RIVER CANYON

Vista-Dome Views

Thrills Galore!
when you travel aboard the

California Zephyr

BURLINGTON · RIO GRANDE · WESTERN PACIFIC

Shooting Stars

Railroads had long appreciated the marketing value of naming their trains, but the aerodynamic styling of the streamliners opened up a rich vein of fresh ideas. The names they gave these sleek new members of the diesel firmament – *Meteors*, *Comets*, *Eagles*, *Zephyrs* – conjured up images of speed, elegance, and glamor, and endowed each train with its distinct personality.

These illuminated drumheads from the New York, New Haven & Hartford's *Comet* (1935) and the Seaboard Air Line's *Silver Meteor* (1939) both invoke astronomical phenomena to create an impression of speed and brilliance.

Right: The New York Central Railroad named its New York-to-Chicago express the *20th Century Limited* as early as 1902, although the name took on a new. Modernist resonance after the train was streamlined by Henry Dreyfuss in 1938.

The New 20TH CENTURY LIMITED

NEW YORK CENTRAL SYSTEM

THE WATER LEVEL ROUTE .... YOU CAN SLEEP

Eagles

The Missouri Pacific's streamliner service acquired its name and emblem in 1939 after the railroad's president, L. W. Baldwin, promised "fame and the thanks of the management" to the employee who came up with the best suggestion. The winning entry, announced in the company magazine, was the *Eagle* – "swift, graceful, powerful and since the creation of our Republic, the symbol of American progress."

Raymond Loewy wrapped a stylized Art Deco eagle of brushed aluminum, emblazoned with MoPac's "buzzsaw" logo, around the noses of the railroad's sleek new EMD diesels and the rear of its observation cars *(left)*. Trackside neon advertisements, timetables, and matchbooks *(overleaf)* promoted the Route of the *Eagles* and dedicated services such as the *Texas Eagle*.

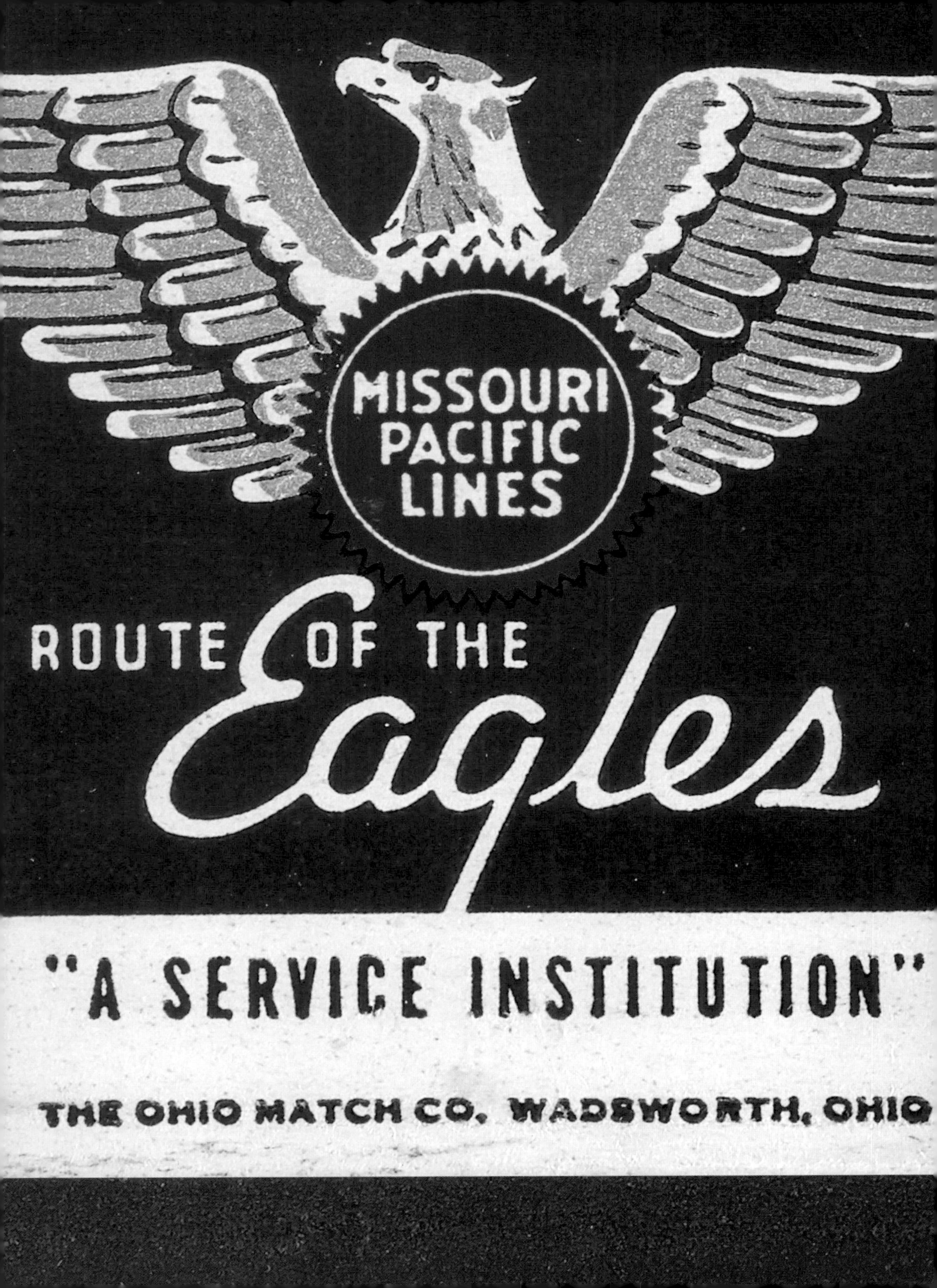
MISSOURI PACIFIC LINES
ROUTE OF THE
Eagles
"A SERVICE INSTITUTION"
THE OHIO MATCH CO. WADSWORTH, OHIO

DEPENDABLE FREIGHT SERVICE

MISSOURI PACIFIC LINES

ROUTE OF THE Eagles

CLOSE COVER BEFORE STRIKING

Zephyrs

BURLINGTON ZEPHYR
AMERICA'S FIRST DIESEL-POWERED
STREAMLINE TRAIN
ENTERED SERVICE NOV. 11, 1934

For more than thirty years the Burlington ran a fleet of streamlined *Zephyr* trains through the Midwest. The routes of these three-car diesels, with their revolutionary stainless-steel bodywork, became known as the Way of the Zephyrs, and the name survives today as an Amtrak service.

The first *Zephyr* of 1934 was renamed the *Pioneer Zephyr* when the fleet expanded. It was retired in 1960 to Chicago's Museum of Science and Industry, where Ian Logan photographed it front, back, and side in the 1970s. When the Burlington introduced new trains drawn by E5 locomotives in 1937, they retained the famous fluted bodywork of the original cars.

Burlington Route

SYSTEM
TIME TABLE

Way of the Zephyrs
AND VISTA-DOMES

The Zephyr Burlington's New Motor Train

DIESEL POWERED
ELECTRICALLY CONTROLLED

A GLEAMING SHAFT OF STAINLESS STEEL

Above and opposite: The promotional
materials for the *Zephyr*'s 1934 launch
stressed the train's clean lines, speed,
and modernity while harking back to
Zephyrus, the god of the west wind
after whom the train was named.

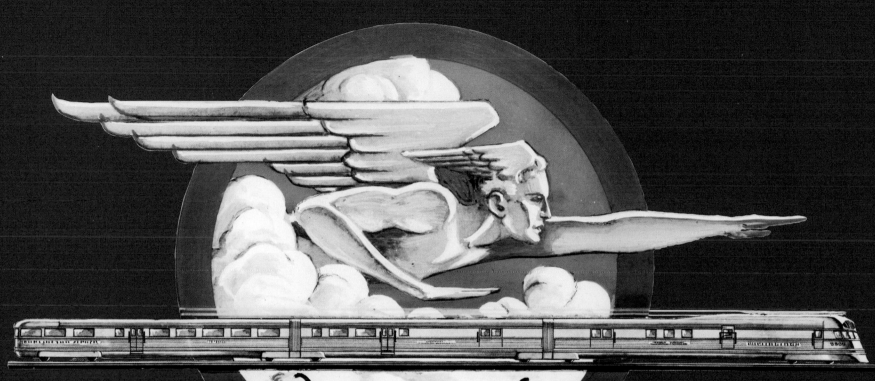

Hiawathas

Drawing inspiration from the Native American cultures of the Upper Midwest, the Milwaukee Road introduced the first of its famous *Hiawathas* on the run from Chicago to Minneapolis in 1935. The sprinting-Indian logo was inspired by Longfellow's poem *The Song of Hiawatha*: "Swift of foot was Hiawatha, He could shoot an arrow from him, And run forward with such fleetness, That the arrow fell behind him." The name *Hiawatha* was not attached to a single train, but was rolled out on a number of routes and used in a plethora of marketing material. It lives on today in an Amtrak service between Chicago and Milwaukee.

The original *Hiawathas* were pulled by streamlined steam locomotives built by Alco and styled by Otto Kuhler, who also designed the passenger cars down the the smallest interior details. The name and brand identity continued after the steam engines were replaced by E6 diesels in 1948.

Morning and Afternoon
Hiawathas

The Aerotrain

Perhaps the most extreme expression of the streamline style was General Motors' futuristic Aerotrain, styled by Chuck Jordan, GM's Chief Designer of Special Projects. Its speed, air-cushioned suspension, and aerodynamic lines were intended to lure passengers away from the airlines, but the train proved extremely noisy, and the ride was hard.

Because the *Aerotrain*'s promise of "air ride comfort" and "striking economies" proved illusory, only two were made. This one, built in 1955, now resides in the Museum of Transportation, Kirkwood, Missouri.

Right: The fluting on the sides of streamlined passenger cars like this Rock Island *Aerotrain* was designed to be aerodynamic while at the same time strengthening the stainless-steel panels.

Interiors

The streamline style was closely related to contemporary developments in architecture, furniture making, and interior design, particularly Art Deco and Modernism. It was applied not only to the exteriors of locomotives and carriages, but also to every aspect of the passenger cars: sleeping compartments, lounges, diners, and cocktail bars. Gone was any attempt to emulate the fusty opulence of a 19th-century hotel or restaurant, replaced by clean lines and modern materials, comfort and convenience. And, just as floor-to-ceiling windows were opening offices and homes to the outside world, glazed observation cars allowed passengers an all-round view of the passing landscape.

Left: The Milwaukee Road introduced the Skytop Lounge, designed by Brooks Stevens, on its *Hiawatha* trains in 1948. The rear of these observation cars was 90 percent glass, affording panoramic views.

Right: When the *Southern Belle* was inaugurated by the Kansas City Southern Railway in 1940, the chromed-steel and leather seats of its Pullman-built observation car were the last word in modern design.

Left: Passengers enjoy the views from the raised observation compartment of a Vista-Dome car.

Above: Union Pacific used matchbooks to tempt passengers into experiencing their high-level observation cars.

Put Yourself Here

in the new
Blue Bird Room
aboard the
Wabash Domeliner
Blue Bird

Join the carefree group in the new "Blue [...] place [...] like lo[...] ments [...] ease! [...] the "B[...] served [...] exclusi[...]

Put Yourself

in one of the *Blue Bird's* four luxurious Domes for an unforgettable new look at mid-America. All *Blue Bird* passengers can enjoy Dome seats—no extra charge.

Put Yourself

in the coach Coffee Shop Club for a light lunch or your favorite soft drink. There's a superb diner and cocktail lounge aboard the *Blue Bird*, too.

ONLY DOME TRAIN BETWEEN CHICAGO AN[...]
Schedules and accommodations shown in Table 1

Left: The Wabash Railroad ran *Blue Bird* express trains between Chicago and St. Louis from 1938 to 1968, introducing the swanky Domeliner in 1950.

Below: After World War II, the New York Central introduced a new range of streamlined aluminum passenger cars, with the emphasis on comfort, modernity, and peace-time optimism.

Right: The Great Northern made the most of its spectacular route over the Rockies by providing short and long domes on its *Empire Builder* trains.

Ready for your first Post-War Vacation . . .

NEW YORK CENTRAL'S
NEW Luxury Coaches

AT last, a long vacation when you can *enjoy* travel more than *ever*. For starting to roll off the production lines right now are New York Central's new luxury coaches, alive with up-to-the-minute travel features hand-picked by more than 5,000 passengers. By summer, many of these superb new cars will be ready to speed you over the Water Level Route at low coach fares . . . on your way to the vacation land of your choice.

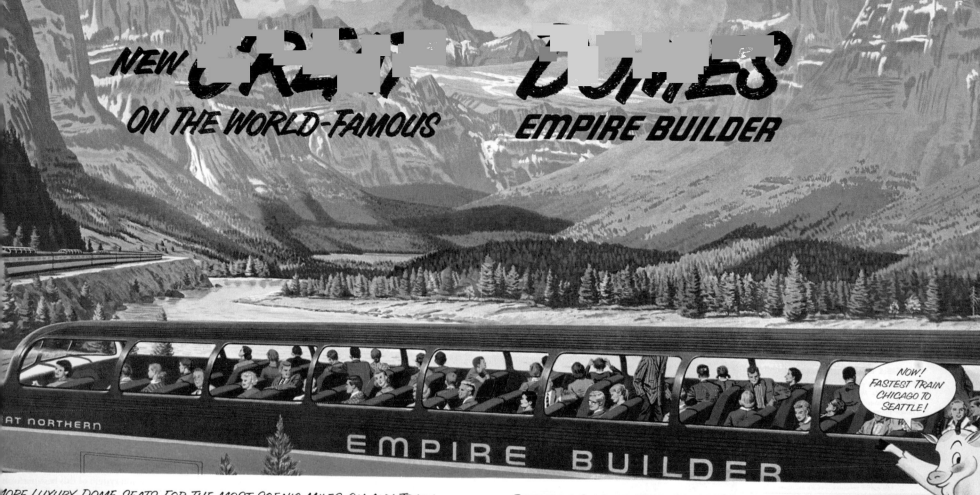

NEW *GREAT DOMES*
ON THE WORLD-FAMOUS **EMPIRE BUILDER**

NOW! FASTEST TRAIN CHICAGO TO SEATTLE!

MORE LUXURY DOME SEATS FOR THE MOST SCENIC MILES ON ANY TRAIN

BETWEEN CHICAGO·TWIN CITIES·SPOKANE·SEATTLE·PORTLAND

GO GREAT...GO GREAT NORTHERN

4 GREAT DOMES ON THE *EMPIRE BUILDER*

Long a pacemaker for train travel at its finest, Great Northern's distinguished Empire Builder now provides 147 topside seats in new Great Dome cars—the most dome seats on any streamliner between Chicago and Pacific Northwest cities.

There now are three luxurious Great Domes in the coach section of the Empire Builder . . . plus an exciting, colorful full-length Great Dome in the Pullman section, with America's smartest lounge on rails on the lower deck.

For a vacation trip of a lifetime . . . for business travel, step aboard the Empire Builder. There's *no extra fare* for helping yourself to a grandstand seat in the Great Domes for the *extra wonderful sightseeing* through Great Northern country.

For information: Write P. G. Holmes, Pass. Traff. Mgr., G. N. Ry., St. Paul 1, Minn.

GO THE GREAT DOME ROUTE
CONNECTIONS TO AND FROM CALIFORNIA

GREAT NORTHERN RAILWAY

Art Deco Typography

The influence of European Modernism that shaped the streamliners also transformed the logos and typography used on the railroads. Out went the ornate lettering that had prevailed since the 19th century, to be replaced by clean sans-serif typefaces that reflected the fast pace of modern life. Many were based on European fonts created in the late 1920s, such as Futura and Kabel. Designed by Paul Renner in Germany in 1927, Futura is characterized by its use of geometric shapes – perfect circles, triangles, and squares – to form the letters and numerals. During the 1930s it became immensely popular and was referred to as "the typeface of today and tomorrow." The lettering designed for the railroads did not correspond exactly to these prototypes, however; what was cast in metal to print on paper did not necessarily look right when applied to a locomotive or passenger or freight car, and the railroads' designers and draftsmen were inventive and precise adapting these originals for use on large surfaces.

Left: A perfect unity of design runs through the 1930s Burlington ticket office in Denver, combining architecture, signboards, and model train window displays.

The Burlington's *Pioneer Zephyr* had striking Art Deco lettering; its thickened stems, lowered crossbars, and squared O echoed the work of the German typographer Lucian Bernhard. The font is likely to have been custom-made by the train's designers Paul Philippe Cret and John Harbeson. *Silver Charger* was the power car of the *General Pershing Zephyr,* the ninth in the fleet.

211

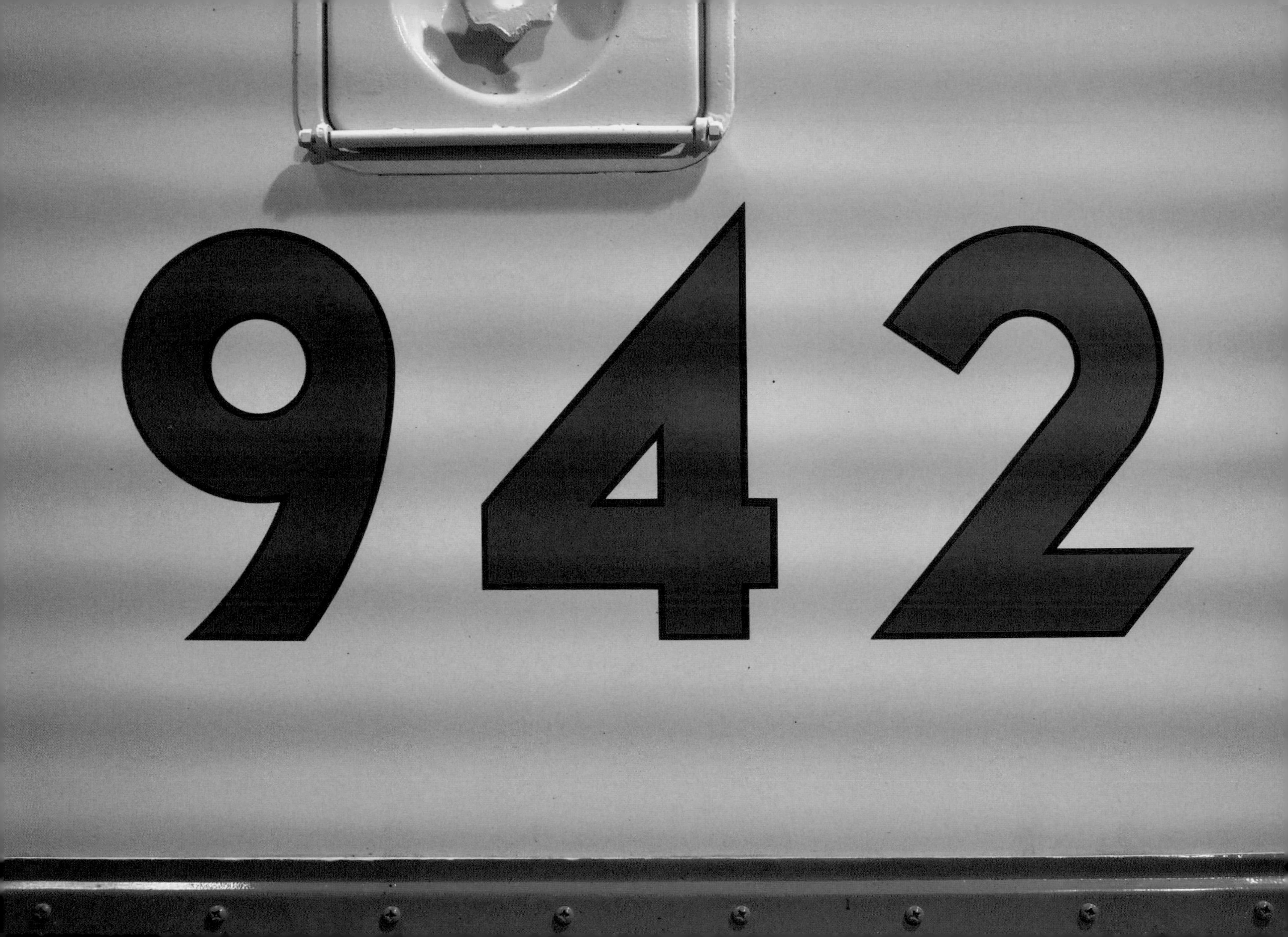
942

Above and left: Although the sans-serif font adopted by Union Pacific in 1939 resembles Futura, it features a number of modifications. The tail of the 9 is squared along the baseline rather than piercing it, while the arm of the 2 has a 45-degree terminal, creating a hint of speed.

Right: The illuminated drumhead of Union Pacific's streamline passenger service *Challenger* uses a condensed version of the company's standard font. The lowered crossbars – not seen elsewhere in the railroad's typography – add a distinctive Art Deco touch.

On the Road

Union Pacific applied the streamline style to its fleet of General Motors PDA (Parlor Diesel Automatic) 4101 coaches in 1948, to compete with its rival Greyhound's Raymond Loewy-styled vehicles.

Photographed along with the rest of the fleet when brand new, the Union Pacific's motorcoach No. 27 has since been restored, and is now kept in the California State Railroad Museum in Sacramento.

6. PHOENIX ARISING

In 1970, President Richard Nixon signed off the federal legislation that gave birth to Amtrak. Few in Washington believed that this quasi-public corporation designed to keep passenger services running on key railway lines was anything other than a short-term proposition. The subsidies the government would need to dish out to keep Nixon's fellow Americans on rails were, in spirit, un-American. No one really expected that passenger railways would pay their way; the consensus was that Americans would turn in ever-increasing numbers to their gas-guzzling cars and fuel-hungry planes, and that the market would soon impose its own logic.

Statistics said it all. Half a century earlier, more than 95 percent of inter-city passenger journeys made in the US were by train. The figure had been as high as 98 percent in 1916, the year before the United States entered World War I. By the time the US joined World War II, it had dropped to 67 percent. The mass-produced automobile had taken its toll. Rail passenger numbers picked up during the war as the US mobilized on a heroic scale, and gas was rationed. They fell quickly as peace and prosperity returned.

Car sales soared, while Greyhound and other long-distance buses came into their own. Frequent flights covered the 960 miles from New York to Chicago in two compared to the sixteen hours by New York Central's finest.

By 1957, just 32 percent of inter-city journeys were made by rail. Despite the high level of service offered by the great Class I railroads and futuristic new trains, money was leaking as if through some mighty transcontinental sieve. Powerful trade unions, antiquated work rules, and fares and rates checked by federal law were other factors damaging the railroads. When in 1968 the US postal service abandoned passenger trains in favor of road and air carriers, the end did indeed seem nigh. One by one the proud names of the past were forced into receivership.

The other sweeping change after 1945 was the disappearance of the great American steam locomotive. Ironically, it began at the very moment when US railroads were building or taking delivery of some of the most powerful and efficient steam engines ever built, among them the New York Central's *Niagara* and the Norfolk

Modern
Coal-Burning
Steam Locomotives
of the
Norfolk and Western
Railway Company

Roanoke, Virginia
September, 1947

A Norfolk & Western brochure illustrates the new J-class streamlined steam locomotive, of which it built fourteen from 1941 to 1950. No. 611 has survived and has been back in steam, running excursions from 1982 to 1994 and again from 2015.

& Western's fleet of streamlined J-Class 4-8-4s. Today, it seems almost incredible that these formidable machines were designed and built not by Alco or General Motors but in Norfolk & Western's own workshops under the direction of its mechanical engineers, Russell G. Henley and John Pilcher, at Roanoke, Virginia. The streamlined casing and livery of Indian red and gold over glossy black were not the work of an outside design consultant such as Raymond Loewy or Henry Dreyfuss, but of Frank Noel, a foreman at Roanoke in charge of constructing passenger cars.

But even as these behemoths were rolling from the sheds, they were increasingly viewed as machines from a vanished age. Their case was hardly helped by the national coal strikes of 1946–47. John L. Lewis, leader of the miners' unions, was – it has been said many times since – the true hero of the diesel lobby by ensuring that there was little or no coal for America's steam locomotives. At the same time, a zealous anti-steam lobby, led by a new breed of Ivy League and business school-educated railroad executives who wanted to be seen as no-nonsense, cost-cutting men of their times, was spreading the gospel of diesel. The cull was swift and draconian. By May 1952, diesel-electric locomotives outnumbered their steam counterparts.

On April Fool's Day, 1958, Stuart T. Saunders, a Harvard-educated lawyer, replaced Robert "Racehorse" Smith as president of the much-loved Norfolk & Western. Sweeping his new broom, Saunders settled on January 1st, 1960 as the date by which steam had to go. If this meant scrapping superb six- and seven-year-old mainline locomotives and even hiring diesels from other railroads to make the point that steam was simply passé, then so be it. By 1961 there were no steam locomotives at work on Class I US railroads.

Saunders represented the race away from economic and cultural regionalism towards global corporatism. When Amtrak opened for business on May 1st, 1971, running passenger services for some twenty bankrupt or otherwise financially exhausted railways, its trains adopted a new corporate identity with a red, white, and blue arrow logo created by the New York advertising agency Lippincott & Margulies, known for its work with Coca-Cola, Pizza Hut, and Dairy Queen. In 2000, this was replaced by a sinuous new logo by the brand consultancy O+CO.

And yet, if the romantic old railroad names, liveries, and logos now seemed the stuff of history, the increase in the number of rail passengers would have surprised President Nixon and politicians in Washington. From 16.6 million in 1971, Amtrak ridership rose to 31.7 million in 2017. If the half billion or so commuter journeys to and from major cities are included, US train ridership was the tenth largest in the world – far below that of intensely rail-minded countries such as Japan, India, Germany, Switzerland, and the UK, yet, despite official predictions, still on the rise.

There had been several factors at work, not least the 1973 oil crisis, when OPEC nations limited oil production and supply to countries – notably the US – that had supported Israel during the Yom Kippur War with Egypt. In a trice, the big, classic all-American car with its insatiably thirsty V8 engine became a liability. The vision of families bowling along interstate highways at ten miles to the gallon dimmed.

The 1980 Staggers Act – named after Harley O. Staggers, chairman of the House Committee on Energy and Commerce – handed the rail industry a lifeline, deregulating prices and freeing companies to sell off unprofitable lines, which became new regional and

short-line railroads. It also led to further mergers, reducing the number of Class I railroads to the present eight. Since then, rising fuel prices, an increasing concern for the environment, traffic congestion on urban roads and, for the young, a growing disenchantment with the car have helped to increase passenger rail travel. Others include a new generation of European-style high-speed trains up and down the East Coast and, to an extent, 9/11. After the terrorist attack on the Twin Towers of the World Trade Center in September 2001, there were those who thought better of boarding an inter-city jet and considered the train a safer option.

Yet despite overcrowding on planes and the sheer unpleasantness of the airport experience, most rail traffic remains local. Amtrak operates fourteen long-distance passenger services, including the sleek *Acela* high-speed trains from Boston to New York and Washington, DC, but these hardly match the style, elegance, and sheer visual appeal of the great trains of the New York Central, Southern Pacific, and Santa Fe.

In recent years, and bit by bit, some of this lost American railroad glory has been revived. The Norfolk & Western J-Class 611 steam locomotive has been restored to working order, as have other mainline locomotives. The extensive, powerful, and profitable Union Pacific long ago gave up nearly all its passenger services, but its freight trains remain a glorious sight as they roll across vast tracts of territory between the Mississippi and the Pacific Ocean. Armour Yellow paintwork. Crisp graphics. That famous UP shield.

The Union Pacific has recently restored one of its 1940s Big Boy fast freight 4-8-8-4 steam locomotives, an immensely powerful and surprisingly fleet machine designed to pull huge freight trains up the long, steep mountain gradients between Ogden, Utah and Cheyenne, Wyoming, cresting Sherman Hill (elevation 8,013 feet) on the way. In its heyday, this articulated machine could be likened to a mobile thunderstorm or a 300-pound marathon runner. A mechanical wonder, it was the star of the Union Pacific's own soulful film *Big Boy: Last of the Giants*, made in 1959 to mourn its passing. Now, Americans and visitors from all over the world can get to see a Big Boy in full cry once again.

Across America, families and enthusiasts have been able to revel in rides through special landscapes by restored steam trains. The Cass Scenic Railroad in West Virginia climbs a switchback former lumber line up to the wonderfully named Bald Knob peak (4,843 feet) using a fleet of rare and sure-footed Shay-geared steam locomotives, mountain goats of the mechanical world. Elsewhere the Durango & Silverton's 1925 vintage Baldwin K-36 2-8-2s wind through pine-covered mountains and along the Animas river on a forty-two-mile line built by the Denver & Rio Grande to bring silver and gold down from the San Juan mountains.

Meanwhile the T1 Trust, a group of steam enthusiasts, is busy recreating a Pennsylvania Railroad T1 4-4-4-4, one of the short-lived yet supremely fast and charismatic shark-nosed 1940s express passenger locomotives styled by Raymond Loewy. Scheduled for completion in 2030, the replica T1 may yet break *Mallard*'s steam speed record.

Occasionally, railroad executives have proven to be true railway enthusiasts. In 1995, Michael Haverty, president of the Kansas City Southern, revived the *Southern Belle* as a business train for freight shippers and guests to ride. This lightweight yellow, green, and red diesel-hauled Kansas City Southern Pullman was originally launched with the help of a beaming Miss Southern Belle, Margaret Landry, in 1940. Haverty bought period GM-EMD diesels from Canada, and had the train painted in authentic heritage livery. A fourth-generation railroader who first worked as a switchman and brakeman for the Missouri Pacific, Haverty believed American railroads need not lose their character nor give up on their heritage as they rode the rails into a new century.

Rust to Rust

In his travels across America in the 1970s, Ian Logan encountered abandoned boxcars and locomotives wherever he went. "This train's got the disappearing railroad blues," wrote Steve Goodman in "The City of New Orleans," the famous song celebrating the morning and evening expresses of the Illinois Central. Almost overnight, those great long-distance trains stopped rumblin' by, a few lingering under Amtrak, others consigned to the memories of "the old men in the club car." Thus forlornly ended a hundred years of American transport history.

An early 0-4-0 steam locomotive awaiting restoration at Montgomery, Alabama *(above left)*, a Pacific Fruit Express refrigerated car decaying beside the tracks in Salinas Valley, California *(right)*, a Kansas City Southern billboard abandoned in a yard in St. Louis *(below left)* – these are some of the relics you could stumble across in the 1970s. Everywhere rust was eating at the names of fallen flags *(overleaf)*.

mo-pac

WESTERN
FEATHER RIVER
ROUTE
PACIFIC

SEABOARD
THROUGH
THE HEART
OF THE
SOUTH
AIR
LINE
RAILROAD

SOUTHERN
SP
PACIFIC

Romance Revived

The demise of passenger rail did not go unlamented. If most Americans found road or air faster and more practical, many missed the adventure of a train journey. To cater for such yearnings and preserve a slice of US history, small railroads sprang up all over the country.

Founded in 1963 by F. Norman Clark to "bring the romance and color of steam railroading back to America," the Roaring Camp Railroad in Felton, California has restored two Shay locomotives to carry visitors on its narrow-gauge track through redwood forests into the Santa Cruz Mountains. It is one of many. In all 2,000 steam engines are in action across the nation, restored and maintained largely by volunteers, aided by engineering firms that still have the tools and skills to repair machinery and rolling stock dating from the 1940s and before.

For those captivated by the magic and mystery of vintage American railroad travel, the experience is still there for the taking.

Above: Shay engines were geared locomotives designed by the logger Ephraim Shay (1839–1916) to haul heavy loads on steep gradients. The Roaring Camp Railroad's *Sonora* is a salvaged three-truck, 60-ton Shay built in 1911 by the Lima works in Ohio.

Right: Based in Cheyenne, Wyoming, Wasatch Railroad Contractors specialize in the restoration of historic rolling stock. Here, a craftsman paints lettering onto a vintage Denver & Rio Grande Western caboose.

Left: On the East Coast, a section of the long-defunct Cape Cod Railroad was revived in 1999 as the Cape Cod Central, running an excursion train of restored vintage cars from Hyannis to Buzzards Bay in all but the winter months.

Right: In 1995, the Kansas City Southern, long given over to freight, reintroduced its *Southern Belle* passenger train as a hospitality service for its business customers. It later extended its classic Brunswick green, red, and gold livery to its freight locomotives, a contemporary salute to a proud past.

Heritage Line Logos

Many heritage railways have created new logos expressive of local tradition and the romance of the past. Unlike the logos of business-oriented railroads designed to project speed, power, and efficiency, they are often whimsical or even humorous.

DURANGO & SILVERTON
NARROW GAUGE RAILROAD & MUSEUM™

SKUNK TRAIN
THE REDWOOD ROUTE – EST. 1885

COLEBROOKDALE · RAILROAD · COMPANY

OREGON COAST SCENIC RAILROAD

MT RAINIER RAILROAD AND LOGGING MUSEUM

WHITE PASS & YUKON ROUTE
GATEWAY TO THE YUKON

New Identities

The profound changes undergone by the US rail network in the 1960s and 1970s were reflected in the visual imagery. As railroad companies amalgamated, new logos replaced old ones, and there were fewer of them. The Amtrak symbol superseded those of the Richmond, Fredericksburg & Potomac, the Seaboard Coast Line, the Burlington Northern and seventeen other passenger services taken over by the corporation. The Penn Central logo, which had supplanted those of the Pennsylvania Railroad and the New York Central, was itself replaced by the logo of Conrail, which was in turn absorbed into the CSX Corporation.

The new emblems were strikingly different from their predecessors. Whereas the original heralds had often been devised by railroad employees such as ticket agents and engineering draftsmen, the task was now entrusted to specialist designers. The groundbreaking work of Allan Fleming, who revolutionized the branding of the Canadian National, set the tone for what followed: clean, businesslike, modern. And while the old symbols and lettering were hand-painted or stenciled directly onto the trains, logos, livery stripes, and other signage were now screen-printed onto self-adhesive vinyl, creating greater uniformity.

Occasionally, old logos were incorporated into a new one. The Genesee & Wyoming Railroad's crisp 1970s logo, for example, had a central space into which each of its subsidiaries could insert a stylized version of their old symbol.

In 2000 Amtrak introduced a new logo featuring a stylized image of rails running through a rolling landscape, called the Travelmark.

Logo Revolution
New Haven

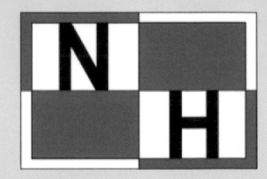

One of the most radical redesigns in US railroad history was the replacement of the New York, New Haven & Hartford's florid Victorian lettering with a crisp Modernist monogram by Herbert Matter. In 1954, Lucille McGinnis, wife of the company president and an interior decorator herself, persuaded her husband that the railroad needed a fresh new image. She commissioned a friend, the furniture designer Florence Knoll, to take on the job. Knoll asked Matter, who was already designing catalogues for Knoll Associates, to create a new logo. The result marked a new era in railroad graphics.

Herbert Matter experimented with scores of designs before arriving at the stacked NH logo that was finally unveiled, in a red and black scheme color scheme, in 1955. After Patrick McGinnis moved to the Boston & Maine in 1956, Matter designed a striking new logo for that railroad as well.

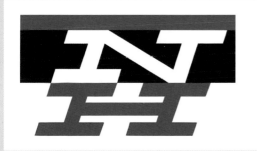

Canadian National

Except for the addition of the patriotic maple leaf during World War II, the Canadian National Railway's classic herald, with its bold underscored type, remained fundamentally unchanged for thirty-six years from its introduction in 1923. But after a 1959 survey revealed that the public thought the railway old-fashioned and change-averse, Dick Wright, its head of public relations, commissioned the New York designer James Valkus to overhaul its image.

Valkus put the young Canadian designer Allan Fleming on the case. After a number of experiments, Fleming sketched out an idea on a cocktail napkin during a flight to New York. "Allan, Make thinner & we've got it," Valkus scribbled on the sketch. The result was a ground-breaking, much imitated logo that has endured for half a century.

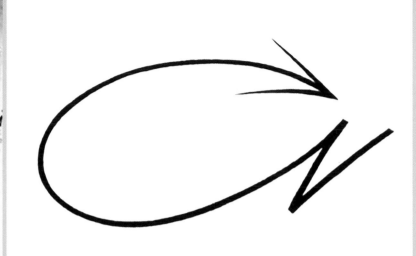

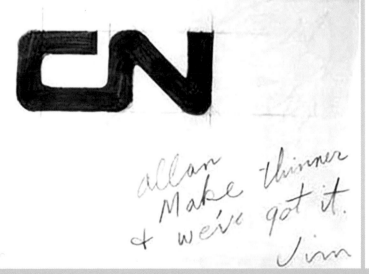

I ♥ G & W

When Mortimer B. Fuller III took control of the Genesee & Wyoming Railroad in 1977, he breathed new life into the company his great-grandfather had founded almost eighty years earlier. Among his first acts was to commission Milton Glaser, the legendary designer of the I ♥ NY logo, to create a symbol for the company that was "at once nostalgic and contemporary."

As the business expanded, acquiring many other short-line railroads, the graphic was adapted to suit them, often incorporating elements of their former logos while maintaining the overall brand identity.

a Genes

GENESEE G&W WYOMING

APALACHICOLA A&N NORTHERN

ALABAMA A GR GULF COAST

WIREGRASS WAC CENTRAL

Business Attire

The later decades of the 20th century saw railroad logos in a state of flux. Canadian Pacific, Rock Island, and the Florida East Coast all got a modern makeover, while Western Pacific's feather symbol was radically simplified. Burlington Northern's dynamic interlocking monogram was in use from 1970 until it merged with the Santa Fe in 1996 to form BNSF, one of the largest freight carriers in North America.

Formed in 1980 out of the merger of the Southern Railway and the Norfolk & Western, the Norfolk Southern is another of the great freight carriers of the US; the horse's head was superimposed onto the initials and speed lines of its logo in 1982. And after CSX absorbed several other carriers, a new logo was designed using the multiplication symbol X and a distinctive chunky font created by the designer and typographer Herb Lubalin.

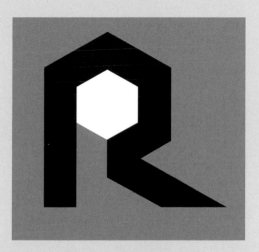

Flying the Flag

In the wake of the attacks of September 11th, 2001, Union Pacific introduced its patriotic new "Building America" livery, with a huge decal of the Stars and Stripes applied to the classic Armour Yellow of its locomotives, matching its familiar shield.

Today's logos are usually applied as screen-printed, self-adhesive vinyl stickers. At Jenks Shop, North Little Rock, Arkansas carmen affix the US flag and Union Pacific shield to a General Electric Evolution Series 44AC. The waving banner (*right*) makes a powerful impression in motion.

FRONT-WINDOW VIEW

A Journey with Ian Logan on the Union Pacific

Chicago – Omaha – Denver – Cheyenne – Laramie – Salt Lake City – Reno – Sacramento – San Francisco

One glimpse of a US railroad train was enough to seal a lifelong passion. On the day of my first encounter with the Rock Island Lines, back in 1968, I vowed to return and document the gutsy graphics on the sides of freight cars, on the noses of locomotives, on benches in stations – everywhere they could be found. In 1975 I spent five weeks traveling across the USA, starting in New York where I wanted to explore the 60th Street freight yard. I wandered around looking for it, found it, and simply walked in. Locomotives were moving up and down the tracks, but no one took any notice of me. I spent a couple of hours there, photographing the logos on the sides of trains. My original plan was to fly on to California to photograph the Vernon Yard in Los Angeles, but on the spur of the moment I thought, I wonder if it's possible to go by train. So I called the Union Pacific office. "If you can get to Chicago this evening," they told me, "we can put you on one of the trains going over, and you can ride in the cab."

I ran to the airport and got a flight to Chicago. It was December, and when I arrived it was twenty degrees below. The wonderful Union Station was cocooned in ice, though there was a giant fire raging in one of the blocks opposite. A fire truck was spraying water on the half burnt-out building. The water froze almost as soon as it left the firemen's hoses, and all the cars were encased in ice where the spray landed. I ran into the station and asked at the ticket office for the *California Zephyr*.

"Oh yes, Mr. Logan, that way."

The train was waiting on the platform, a big yellow diesel locomotive, an SPD40F, I think, with a string of Amtrak passenger cars. I climbed up into the cab with the engineer, and for the next two or three days I traveled across America with a front-window view.

Left: Chicago Union Station, seen a couple of years before I arrived, was designed by Daniel Burnham, the architect of Washington Union Station, and endowed with an equal level of "magic to stir men's souls," to quote Burnham's lofty ambition.

Below: I had an engineer's view of the prairies as we headed across Nebraska after leaving Omaha, headquarters of the Union Pacific. Telegraph poles still marched west beside the tracks, just as they had in the 1860s when the line was built.

The cab had a refrigerator and a banquette so the engineers could take a rest. I slept in one of the passenger cars. When I awoke the next morning, we were on the prairies. Crossing Nebraska was amazing – just miles and miles of flat landscape. You could see the Rockies in the distance, but it seemed to take an age to get to them. At first, the engineer hardly spoke to me. It took me some time to work out that as an Englishman, a designer, I was someone totally outside his frame of reference. As far as he was concerned, I might as well have been a man from Mars.

I remember getting off at Denver, where we stopped for half an hour. A Seaboard Coast Line train had pulled up on the opposite

I photographed an oncoming Union Pacific freight train from the cab of my *California Zephyr* as we rolled across Wyoming.

track, thousands of miles from home, on its way to a railroad museum. I ran across the rails to get a closer look at the classic streamliner E6 loco in its sleek black and yellow livery.

It was snowing as we began the climb into the Rockies, along winding tracks and across bridges over steep gorges. Whenever we stopped, the engineer let me get out and photograph the station.

As we were coming into a town one morning, I could see cowboys on horseback. I couldn't believe this was the 1970s, not the 1870s. I asked him, "Where is this?" and he said, "Cheyenne." I asked him why they were on horseback. "It's a cow town," he said. "There's big stock yards here."

By then we'd started talking, and as we were coming into the station he looked at me and said, "D'ya wanna pull the horn?"

I was thrilled to bits. I nearly fell over in my rush to get across the cab. Taking hold of the rope that hung from the roof, I pulled. The air horn above us gave a huge blast. It's a wonderful sound. You can hear it from miles away. I had a tape recorder with me and made a recording to play to friends later.

After the engineer granted me the honor of pulling the horn, I got chatting to him. I asked him if it was true that Union Pacific engineers were given a gold stopwatch as a reward for long service. He said he didn't know anything about that. But a few hours later I saw him pull a big gold watch from his pocket to time the distance between the mileposts. *(continued on page 254)*

We are held at a red signal as we prepare to descend a steep gradient.

Across the prairies, snowy mountains appeared, heralding the ascent into the Rockies.

The mountain landscape is never so dramatic as when seen from the engineer's cab, with telegraph poles snaking over the rocks.

"So, you do have one," I said.

"Yep, it was my grandaddy's," he replied.

People who work on the railroad are all families. From grandfather to father to son, their service goes back generations. It was then that I realized I had been intruding. I was somebody from outside, sharing the little secrets railroaders keep to themselves. It's slightly embarrassing to some of them to have an outsider enter their close-knit community. The volunteers who staff the railroad historical societies today are all ex-railroaders and they are very dedicated to the lines they worked on, years after the companies ceased to exist as separate entities.

We changed engineers after Salt Lake City. The second engineer woke me up at around 3 a.m. He wanted to show me that we were traveling down a street in Reno; the tracks were laid right along the road, with buildings on either side. The town was ablaze with light, and there were still a few people wandering between the gambling halls. I realized then that the railroads were there first and the towns grew up around the tracks.

We came down from the Sierra Nevada through Sacramento and eventually arrived in San Francisco. At that time, the railroad ran along the waterfront. The station on Third and Townsend, where some friends met me, was a wonderful building in the Spanish mission style. The wooden seats in the main hall had the Southern Pacific logo carved into them. Just six months after I was there, the station was pulled down and the tracks taken up; trains now terminate in Oakland. The glory days of the American passenger trains were fading into the past, and I was lucky to have made this fantastic journey while it was still possible.

Railroad Patches

In the course of his travels, Ian Logan became an avid collector of fabric patches incorporating the logos of railroads such as the Union Pacific, the Santa Fe, and the Frisco. Some are originals worn on the uniforms of train drivers, mechanics, and maintenance staff; others are replicas manufactured for railway enthusiasts.

A Railroad Glossary

0-4-0, 2-6-0, 4-6-2, etc.: Devised by Frederick Methvan Whyte, an employee of the New York Central Railroad, in the early 1900s, the Whyte system classifies locomotives according to their wheel configuration. The first figure is the number of leading wheels, the second the number of driving wheels, and the third the number of trailing wheels.

Air line: 19th-century term for the shortest distance between two points. The Seaboard Air Line Railway ran (almost) "straight as a plumb line" from Washington, DC to Tampa, Florida.

Alco: American Locomotive Company. One of the leading US steam locomotive builders, Alco operated from 1901 to 1969 in Schenectady, New York.

Baldwin Locomotive Works: major US steam locomotive builder based in Philadelphia from 1825 to 1906, and then at Eddystone, Pennsylvania until it went out of business in 1956.

Billboard: dark-blue and yellow livery adopted by the Santa Fe in the 1960s.

Boxcar: enclosed freight car of wood or steel with sliding doors in the sides.

Caboose: car attached to the rear of a freight train to serve as an office for the conductor and trainmen; will have either a glazed cupola on the roof or bay windows in the sides to allow the crew to view the full length of the train.

Class I, II, and III railroads: Since 1911, US railroads have been classified according to their operating revenue, with the thresholds regularly adjusted for inflation. In general, Class I covers transcontinental and major regional railroads, Class II other regional railroads, and Class III short-line, local railroads.

Cog railway: also rack or rack-and-pinion railway. A railway designed for steep gradients, where the locomotives are fitted with cogwheels that engage with a toothed rack between the rails.

Drive wheel: wheel, driven by pistons and rods, that propels the locomotive.

Drumhead: illuminated sign, usually bearing the railroad company logo, that could be mounted on the rear of passenger trains.

E locomotives: series of streamlined diesel passenger locomotives built by the EMD, starting with the E1 in 1937 and concluding with the E9, introduced in 1954. The E stood for eighteen hundred horsepower, though later models were more powerful.

F locomotives: series of diesel-electric locomotives built by the EMD from 1939 to 1960. The F stood for fourteen hundred horsepower.

EMD: Electro-Motive Division of General Motors, a major builder of diesel-electric locomotives based in the Chicago suburb of La Grange, Illinois.

Engineer: the driver of a locomotive.

Flatcar: open freight car used to transport containers or loads that are too large for a standard boxcar.

Gauge: width of railroad track. US standard gauge is 4 feet 8½ inches.

GP: series of General Purpose roadswitchers built by General Motors' Electro-Motive Division (EMD) between 1949 and 1990.

Herald: railroad company logo.

Hopper: freight car with a sloping floor to allow a load such as grain to discharge by gravity once the doors are opened.

Hump yard: marshalling yard where cars are pushed up a raised hump by a switcher engine, and allowed to roll down under the force of gravity as they are routed to the correct track.

The Burlington's streamlined, all-stainless-steel *Zephyr*, seen here at La Crosse, Wisconsin entered service in 1934 between Kansas City and Lincoln, Nebraska.

Rack railway: see cog railway.

Reefer: refrigerated boxcar.

Reporting mark: two- to four-letter code stenciled onto every locomotive and car on the US system to identify its owner.

Roadswitcher: locomotive that could be used both to haul trains out on the railroads and shunt ("switch") cars in yards.

Shay engine: locomotive built to a design patented by the logger Ephraim Shay (1839–1916), which transmitted power to the wheels via gears, enabling it to pull heavy loads up steep gradients.

Streamline: aerodynamic style, often combining elements of Art Deco and Modernism, applied to locomotives and passenger cars from the 1930s.

Switcher: locomotive designed for moving railroad cars in yards and terminals. Known as a shunting engine in the UK.

Tender: car pulled behind a steam locomotive to carry fuel and water.

Warbonnet: red and silver livery introduced in 1937 on the Santa Fe *Super Chief*.

Lima Locomotive Works: steam engine builder based in Lima, Ohio from 1877, best known for the manufacture of Shay geared locomotives.

Limited train: express service stopping at only a limited number of stations, e.g. New York Central's *20th Century Limited.*

Livery: paint scheme applied to locomotives and rolling stock – a major, instantly identifiable element in a railroad's branding.

Pay car: railroad car used as a mobile cashier's office to dispense wages to employees along the line.

Piggyback: carriage on railroad flat cars of wheeled freight trailers that can also be hitched to trucks for transport by road.

Pullman: based in Chicago, the company founded by George Pullman in 1862 built luxury passenger and sleeping cars until its demise in 1969.

Railroad Names, Abbreviations, and Nicknames

The name of each railroad mentioned in this book is followed by its initials, where used, or reporting mark (often the same), and any nickname or other epithet applied to it.

Amtrak (National Railroad Passenger Corporation), AMTZ

Alabama & Gulf Coast Railway, AGR

Apalachicola Northern Railroad, AN

Atchison, Topeka & Santa Fe Railway, AT&SF, Santa Fe

Atlantic Coast Line Railroad, ACL

Atlantic, Mississippi & Ohio, AM&O

Baltimore & Ohio Railroad, B&O

Boston & Maine Railroad, B&M

Burlington Northern Santa Fe Railway, BNSF, Burlington

Burlington & Northern, B&N

Butte & Plumas Railway

California Western Railroad, CWR, Skunk Train

Canadian National, CN

Canadian Pacific Railway, CP

Cape Cod Central Railroad, CCCR

Carroll Park & Western Railroad, CP&W

Cass Scenic Railroad

Central of Georgia Railway, CG, Route of Nancy Hanks

Central Pacific Railroad, CPRR

Chesapeake & Ohio Railroad, C&O, Chessie System

CSX, CSXT, Chessie-Seaboard

Chicago, Burlington & Quincy Railroad, CBQ, Burlington Route

Chicago & Eastern Illinois, CEI

Chicago & Illinois Midland Railway, C&IM

Chicago, Milwaukee, St. Paul & Pacific Railroad, CMStP&P, Milwaukee Road

Chicago & North Western Transportation Company, CNW, North Western

Chicago, Rock Island & Pacific Railroad, RI, Rock Island Lines, The Rock

Cleveland, Cincinnati, Chicago & St. Louis Railway, CCC&StL, The Big Four

Colebrookdale Railroad

Colorado Midland Railway, CM, Midland Route

Delaware & Hudson Railway, D&H

Delaware, Lackawanna & Western Railroad, DL&W, Lackawanna/Route of Phoebe Snow

Denver & Rio Grande Railroad, DRG, Rio Grande/Scenic Line of the World

Durango & Silverton Narrow Gauge Railroad, D&SNG

Florida East Coast Railway, FEC, Overseas Railroad

Genesee & Wyoming, G&W

Georgia Railroad & Banking Company, GA, Georgia Rail/Old Reliable

Great Northern Railway, GN, Route of the Empire Builder

Great Smoky Mountains Railroad, GSM

Gulf Mobile & Ohio Railroad, GM&O, GeeMo

Gulf, Mobile & Northern Railroad, GM&N, Road of Service

Illinois Central Gulf Railroad, ICG

Illinois Central Railroad, IC, Main Line of Mid-America

Kansas City Southern Railway, KCS, Route of the Southern Belle

Kiamichi Railroad, KRR

Long Island Rail Road, LIRR, Route of the Dashing Commuter

Louisville & Nashville Railroad, L&N, Dixie Line

Manitou & Pikes Peak Railway, MPP, Pikes Peak Cog Railway

Minneapolis, St. Paul & Sault Ste. Marie Railroad, SOO, Soo Line

Missouri-Kansas-Texas Railway, MKT/KT, Katy Line

Missouri Pacific Railroad, MP, MoPac /Route of the Eagles

Mount Rainier Railroad, MRRR

Mount Tamalpais & Muir Woods Railway, The Crookedest Railroad in the World

Nashville, Chattanooga & St. Louis Railway, NC&StL, Dixie Line

New York Central Railroad, NYC

New York, Chicago & St. Louis , NYC&StL, Nickel Plate Road

New York, New Haven & Hartford Railroad, NH, New Haven

Niles Canyon Railway

Norfolk & Petersburg Railroad, N&P

Norfolk Southern Railway, NS

Norfolk & Western Railway, N&W, King Coal

Northern Pacific Railway, NP, Route of the Great Big Baked Potato

Northwestern Pacific Railroad, NWP, Redwood Empire Route

Oregon Coast Scenic Railroad, OCSR

Pennsylvania Railroad, PRR, Pennsy

Penn Central Transportation Company, PC

Pikes Peak Cog Railway, see Manitou & Pikes Peak Railway

Richmond, Fredericksburg & Potomac Railroad, RFP

Roaring Camp & Big Trees Narrow Gauge Railroad

Sacramento Northern Railway, SN

SAM Short Line

Seaboard Air Line Railroad, SAL, Route of Courteous Service

Seaboard Coast Line Railroad, SCL

South Side Railroad

Southern Pacific Railroad, SP, Espee

Southern Railway, SOU/SR

Spokane, Portland & Seattle Railway, SPS

St. Louis-San Francisco Railway, SLSF, Frisco

St. Louis Southwestern Railway, SSL, Cotton Belt Route

Tallulah Falls Railway, TF, TF and Huckleberry

Texas State Railroad, TS

Union Pacific Railroad, UP, Overland Route

Virginia & Tennessee Railroad, V&T

Wabash Railroad, WAB, Banner Line

Western & Atlantic Railroad, W&A, State Road

Western Maryland Railway, WM

Western Pacific Railroad, WP, Feather River Route

White Pass & Yukon Route, Gateway to the Yukon

Wiregrass Central Railroad, WGCR

Select Bibliography

Blaszak, Michael W. & Gruber, John, *Chicago: America's Railroad Capital*. Voyageur Press, Minneapolis, MN, 2014.

Bradley, Glenn D., *The Story of the Santa Fe*. Gorham Press, Boston, MA, 1920.

Bruce, Alfred W., *The Steam Locomotive in America: Its Development in the Twentieth Century*. Bonanza, New York, 1952.

Byron, Carl R., *The Pioneer Zephyr: America's First Diesel-Electric Stainless Steel Streamliner*. Heimburger House, Forest Park, IL, 2006.

Cook, Richard J. Sr., *The Twentieth Century Limited 1938–1967*. TLC Publishing, Lynchburg, VA, 1993.

Cooper, Bruce Clement (ed.), *The Classic Western American Railroad Routes*. Chartwell Books, New York, 2010.

Ellis, C. Hamilton, *Railways: A Pictorial History of the First 150 Years*. Peebles, New York, 1974.

Glischinski, Steve, *Santa Fe Railway*. MBI Publishing, Osceola, WI, 1997.

Gottfried, Herbert, *Erie Railway Tourist, 1854–1886: Transporting Visual Culture*. Lehigh University Press, Bethlehem, PA, 2018.

Grant, H. Roger, *Railroads and the American People*. Indiana University Press, Bloomington, IN, 2012.

Follow the Flag: A History of the Wabash Railroad Company. DeKalb, IL: Northern Illinois University Press, 2004.

The North Western: A History of the Chicago & North Western Railway. Northern Illinois University Press, DeKalb, IL, 1996.

Royal Blue Line: The Classic B&O Train Between Washington and New York. Johns Hopkins University Press, Baltimore, MD, 2002.

Hayes, Derek, *Historical Atlas of the North American Railroad*. University of California Press, Oakland, CA, 2010.

Klein, Maury, *Unfinished Business: The Railroad in American Life*. University Press of New England, Lebanon, NH, 1994.

Union Pacific (3 vols). Doubleday, New York, 1987, 1990; Oxford University Press, New York, 2011.

Krebs, Robert D., *Riding the Rails: Inside the Business of America's Railroads*. Indiana University Press, Bloomington, IN, 2018.

Lamb, J. Parker, *Katy: Diesels to the Gulf*. Andover Junction Publications, Mendota, IL, 1991.

Link, O. Winston & Hensley, Tim, *Steam, Steel & Stars: America's Last Steam Railroad*. Abrams, New York, 1987.

Lovegrove, Keith, *Railway: Identity, Design and Culture*. Laurence King, London, 2004.

Middleton, William D., Smerk, George M. & Diehl, Roberta L. (eds), *Encyclopedia of North American Railroads*. Indiana University Press, Bloomington, IN, 2007.

Nock, O. S., *Railways of the USA*. A. & C. Black, London, 1979.

Orsi, Richard J., *Sunset Limited: The Southern Pacific Railroad and the Development of the American West, 1850–1930*. University of California Press, Oakland, CA, 2005.

Potter, Janet Greenstein, *Great American Railroad Stations*. Wiley, New York, 1996.

Reynolds, William, *European Capital, British Iron, and an American Dream: The Story of the Atlantic & Great Western Railroad*. University of Akron Press, Akron, OH, 2002.

Schneider, Gregory L., *Rock Island Requiem: The Collapse of a Mighty Fine Line*. University Press of Kansas, Lawrence, KS, 2013.

Schwantes, Carlos A., *Railroad Signatures across the Pacific Northwest*. University of Washington Press, Seattle, WA, 1993.

Scribbins, Jim, *The Hiawatha Story*. Kalmbach Publishing, Waukesha, WI, 1970.

Solomon, Brian, *North American Railroads: The Illustrated Encyclopedia*. Voyageur Press, Minneapolis, MN, 2014.

Acknowledgements

Stilgoe, John R., *Metropolitan Corridor: Railroads and the American Scene. Yale University Press*, New Haven, CT, 1983.

Stover, John F., *The Life and Decline of the American Railroad.* Oxford University Press, New York, 1970.

Vance, James E., *The North American Railroad: Its Origin, Evolution, and Geography.* Johns Hopkins University Press, London, 1995.

White, Richard, *Railroaded: The Transcontinentals and the Making of Modern America.* W. W. Norton, New York, 2011.

Withuhn, William L., *American Steam Locomotives: Design and Development, 1880–1960.* Indiana University Press, Bloomington, IN, 2019.

Wolmar, Christian, *The Great Railroad Revolution: The History of Trains in America.* Public Affairs, New York, 2012.

Zega, Michael E. & Gruber, John E., *Travel by Train: The American Railroad Poster 1870–1950.* Indiana University Press, Bloomington, IN, 2002.

Zimmerman, Karl R., *20th Century Limited.* MBI Publishing, St. Paul, MN, 2003.

Ian Logan would like to thank the publisher, Simon Rigge, and the editor, Chris Schüler, plus all the staff and interns at Sheldrake Press for their incredible hard work in putting this book together; Jonathan Glancey for his wonderful writing and fantastic enthusiasm; Bernard Higton for his design; Eric Ladd at Pixywalls Ltd. for introducing me to Sheldrake Press; and all the following individuals, societies, museums, and libraries for their help:

American Rails (www.american-rails.com); the Bangor & Aroostook Historical Society; Marty Bernard – a great help; Seth H. Bramson, Company Historian, Florida East Coast Railway; Craig Ordner, Santa Fe Archivist, Temple Railroad and Heritage Museum, Texas; Jessie Durant, Archivist, Santa Cruz Beach Boardwalk Archives; the Erie Lackawanna Railroad Historical Society; Danny Farnsworth; the Flagler Museum Archives, Palm Beach, Florida; Michael Hibblen, broadcaster, Hibblen Radio; David Huelsing of the Missouri Pacific Historical Society; Arthur Huneke for the Long Island Railroad logos; Mike Keim at RailPictures.Net; Douglas Kidd, Rock Island Railroad; Jennifer Davis McDaid, Archivist, Norfolk Southern Corporation; the Nashville Steam Preservation Society; the National Museum of Transportation, St. Louis, Missouri; the National Railway Historical Society; the Nickel Plate Road Historical and Technical Society; the Northwestern Pacific Railroad Historical Society; the Orange Empire Railway Museum; the Railroad Commissary; Roaring Camp Railroad, Felton, California; Mike Schafer, Art Director, White River Productions; Rob Schreiner, Illinois Railway Museum; Alison Seyler and Ryan McPherson, Archivists, B&O Railroad Museum, Baltimore; the Tennessee Central Railway Museum; John Thompson of Kansas City; Allen Tuten of the Central of Georgia Railway Historical Society; and Raymond D. Woods Jnr., Business Manager, Santa Fe Railway Historical and Modeling Society.

Jonathan Glancey would like to thank Ian Logan, whose photographs sparked this entire project, and all the Sheldrake team, who brought it to completion.

Sheldrake Press wish to thank Seth Bramson of the Florida East Coast Railway; Tim Doherty; Matt Donnelly of Amtrak; David R. Godine; Mike Lewis of Wasatch Railroad Contractors; Julie Palermo of American Premier Underwriters; and Laura Walker of the Norfolk Southern Railway. Finally, we would like to thank our Feline Director, Mr. Jenks, for his unwavering committment to the cause (in exchange for a few Dreamies).

Picture Credits

Sources for the illustrations in this book are listed from the top of the left-hand column to the bottom of the right-hand column on each double page.

Front Cover – Neil Gower, Newberry Library, Chicago (Chicago, Burlington & Quincy Railroad Company Records). Back Cover – Ian Logan Collection; Ian Logan; Ian Logan. Endpapers – All by Ian Logan. Frontispiece – Ian Logan. 6/7 – GA/Yukio Futagawa. 8/9 – Ian Logan Collection. 10/11 – Ian Logan Collection; Ian Logan. 12/13 – Ian Logan Collection; Ian Logan Collection, photo in *Inhabit*, 1975. 14/15 Ian Logan Collection. 16/17 – Ian Logan. 18/19 – Library of Congress, Prints and Photographs Division, © George A. Crofutt. 20/21 – Ian Logan Collection. 22/23 – Museums Victoria, Gerald & Lorna Dee Collections; Ian Logan; Museums Victoria, Gerald & Lorna Dee Collections. 24/25 – Both from Ian Logan Collection. 26/27 – Ian Logan. 28/29 – Union Pacific Historical Collection; from *The Sign Painter*, Pullman School of Lettering; Dick Harley Collection. 30/31 – Mike Lewis, Wasatch Railroad Contractors; Newberry Library, Chicago; Newberry Library, Chicago (Chicago, Burlington & Quincy Railroad Company Archives); Marty Bernard. 32/33 – BNSF (the Great Northern Railway mark is a licensed mark owned by BNSF Railway Company); Union Pacific Railroad; Chicago, Rock Island & Pacific Railroad; Canadian National Railway; BNSF (the Santa Fe marks are licensed marks owned by BNSF Railway Company); Union Pacific Railroad; BNSF (the Burlington Route mark is a licensed

mark owned by BNSF Railway Company); BNSF (the Northern Pacific Railway mark is a licensed mark owned by BNSF Railway Company); Union Pacific Railroad; American Premier Underwriters, Inc.; licensed from the Milwaukee Road Historical Association; Union Pacific Railroad. 34/35 – Union Pacific Railroad; Rob Schreiner. 36/37 – Both by Ian Logan. 38/39 – Ian Logan; Roger Puta, Marty Bernard; Ian Logan Collection. 40/45 – All by Ian Logan. 46/47 – Chicago, Rock Island & Pacific Railroad; Ian Logan Collection. 48/49 – Ian Logan. 50/51 – Both from Ian Logan Collection. 52/53 – Ian Logan; Ian Logan Collection; Ian Logan; Ian Logan; 54/55 – Ian Logan Collection; Ian Logan. 56/61 All by Ian Logan. 62/63 Ian Logan Collection. 64/65 – Courtesy of the Broadmoor Archives, Colorado Springs, CO. 66/67 – Ian Logan. 68/69 – Courtesy Myrna and Seth Bramson, Florida East Coast Railway Archive; Library of Congress, Geography and Map Division. 70/71 – CSX Corporation; Norfolk Southern Corp.; CSX Corporation; CSX Corporation; Northwestern Pacific Railroad; CSX Corporation; CSX Corporation; Pan Am Railways, Inc.; CSX Corporation; Norfolk Southern Corp.; CSX Corporation; Colorado and Midland Railway, David Drewry Collection. 72/73 – Both by Ian Logan. 74/75 – Library of Congress, Prints and Photographs Division, LC-USZC4-11778; Conway Scenic Railroad; Paolo Roffo; Benjamin Dziechciowski. 76/77 – Courtesy Myrna and Seth Bramson, Florida East Coast Railway Archive; Ian Logan Collection; Ian Logan Collection. 78/79 – Courtesy Myrna and Seth Bramson, Florida East Coast Railway

Archive; CSX Corporation. 80/81 – Courtesy of the Santa Cruz Beach Boardwalk Archives; courtesy of the Santa Cruz Beach Boardwalk Archives; Ian Logan. 82/83 – All by Ian Logan. 84/85 – Both by Ian Logan. 86/87 – Wabash Railroad Historical Society; Norfolk Southern Corp.; Norfolk Southern Corp. 88/89 – All from Ian Logan Collection. 90/91 – Nickel Plate Road Historical and Technical Society Collection; Ian Logan Collection; Ian Logan Collection; Ian Logan Collection; Ian Logan Collection; Ian Logan Collection. 92/93 – Ian Logan; Ian Logan; CSX Corporation. 94/95 – Marty Bernard; CSX Corporation; photographer unknown, collection of the Central of Georgia Railway Historical Society; Norfolk Southern Corp. 96/97 – Ian Logan Collection; Ian Logan Collection; LIRRer Employee Magazine, April 25, 1963, Dave Morrison Archive; Marty Bernard. 98/99 – All by Ian Logan. 100/101 – Both by Mitch Goldman. 102/103 – Cincinnati Museum Center. 104/105 – Ian Logan Collection; Library of Congress, Prints and Photographs Division. 106/107 – Everett Collection/Mary Evans; Streamlinermemories.info. 108/109 – Ian Logan. 110/111 – Both Ian Logan Collection. 112/113 – Ian Logan. 114/115 – Ian Logan; Adam Smith; Ian Logan; Ian Logan; Ian Logan; Ian Logan; Stuart L. Schroeder; Ian Logan. 116/117 – Library of Congress, Prints & Photographs Division; Ian Logan. 118/119 – Brian Janssen, PicFair; Derek Carter. 120/121 – All Cincinnati Museum Center. 122/123 – Ian Logan Collection; Ian Logan. 124/127 – All by Ian Logan. 128/129 – Tom Farence; Ian Logan. 130/133 – All by Ian Logan.

134/135 – Streamlinermemories.info. 136/137 – Railroad Museum of Pennsylvania, Oversize Archival Collection, PHMC. 138/139 – Ian Logan Collection; Streamlinermemories.info. 140/141 DaTo Images/ Bridgeman Images; courtesy of California State Railroad Museum Library & Archives. 142/143 – Ian Logan Collection; Ian Logan. 144/145 – All Ian Logan Collection. 146/147 – All from the Collections of the B&O Railroad Museum. 148/149 – Railroad Museum of Pennsylvania, Oversize Archival Collection, PHMC; Railroad Museum of Pennsylvania, Oversize Archival Collection, PHMC; courtesy of the Monroe County Historical Association, Stroudsburg, PA. 150/151 – Ian Logan Collection; Ian Logan Collection; Delaware, Lackawanna & Western Railroad, Daniel Carey Collection; courtesy of the Monroe County Historical Association, Stroudsburg, PA. 152/153 – Ian Logan Collection; Ian Logan Collection; Ian Logan Collection; Ian Logan. 154/155 – Ian Logan Collection; Ian Logan Collection; Ian Logan. 156/157 – All by Ian Logan. 158/161- All from Fred M. and Dale M. Springer Archives, Temple, TX. 162/163 – Ian Logan. 164/165 – Union Pacific Railroad; Union Pacific Railroad; Union Pacific Railroad; Union Pacific Railroad; Ian Logan; Ian Logan. 166/167 – All American Premier Underwriters, Inc. 168/169 – Railroad Museum of Pennsylvania, Gladulich Slides, PHMC; American Premier Underwriters, Inc.; American Premier Underwriters, Inc. 170/171 – Nickel Plate Road Historical and Technical Society Collection; Streamlinermemories. info. 172/173 – Streamlinermemories.info;

Streamlinermemories.info; Streamlinermemories.info; Ian Logan; Ian Logan Collection; Ian Logan Collection; Ian Logan Collection. 174/175 – The Huntington Library, Art Museum, and Botanical Gardens. 176/177 – Ian Logan Collection. 178/179 – Cooper-Hewitt, Smithsonian Design Museum, NY, © Photo SCALA, Florence and American Financial Enterprises, Inc., courtesy of Raymond Loewy Foundation; Brighton Toy and Model Museum. 180/181 – CSX Corporation; New York Public Library, the Buttolph Collection of Menus, 1943. 182/183 – SC 1940.18, Charles Sheeler, *Rolling Power*, 1939, oil on canvas, 22 5/8 x 37 5/8 in, purchased with the Drayton Hillyer Fund, Smith College Museum of Art, Northampton, Massachusetts. 184/185 – Both from Ian Logan Collection. 186/187 – CSX Corporation; Ian Logan Collection. 188/189 – All from Ian Logan Collection. 190/191 – Ian Logan; Marty Bernard; The Huntington Library, Art Museum, and Botanical Gardens. 192/193 – James P. Bell; J. Parker Lamb. 194/195 – Ian Logan Collection. 196/197 – Ian Logan; Ian Logan; Ian Logan; Ian Logan Collection. 198/199 – Both from Newberry Library, Chicago (Chicago, Burlington & Quincy Railroad Company Records). 200/201 – Ian Logan Collection; Streamlinermemories.info; Ian Logan. 202/203 – Both by Ian Logan. 204/205 – Streamlinermemories.info; Ian Logan. 206/207 – Ian Logan; Ian Logan Collection. 208/209 – All from Ian Logan Collection. 210/211 – Newberry Library, Chicago (Chicago, Burlington & Quincy Railroad Company Records); Ian Logan; Ian Logan. 212/213 – Ian Logan; Newberry Library, Chicago

(Pullman Digital Collection); Ian Logan. 214/215 – Lisa Elliot; Ian Logan; Ian Logan. 216/217 – Mike Raia. 218/219 – Ian Logan. 220/221 – Ian Logan Collection. 222/223 – National Railroad Passenger Corporation. 224/225 – All by Ian Logan. 226/227 – RailPictures.Net, © Frank Orona; rest by Ian Logan. 228/229 – Ian Logan; Mike Lewis, Wasatch Railroad Contractors. 230/231 – Ian Logan. 232/233 – Niles Canyon Railway; Pacific Southwest Railway Museum; Great Smoky Mountains Railroad; Historic SAM Shortline Railroad; Roaring Camp Railroads; Texas State Railroad; Durango & Silverton Narrow Gauge Railroad; Oregon Coast Scenic Railroad; Skunk Train; Mt. Rainier Railroad and Logging Museum; Colebrookdale Railroad Preservation Trust; White Pass & Yukon Route. 234/235 – brandonkleinvideo, 123rf.com. 236/237 – All logos American Financial Enterprises, Inc.; photo Hot Foot Design. 238/239 – Photo Ian Logan; all logos Canadian National Railway. 240/241 – All from Genesee & Wyoming, Inc. 242/243 – National Railroad Passenger Corporation; Conrail; CSX Corporation; Union Pacific Railroad; BNSF (The Burlington Northern mark is a licensed mark owned by BNSF Railway Company); Canadian Pacific Railway; courtesy Myrna and Seth Bramson, Florida East Coast Railway Archive; Norfolk Southern Corp.; Chicago, Rock Island & Pacific Railroad. 244/245 – Mike Danneman; Mike Danneman; Frank Orona. 246/255 – All by Ian Logan. 256/257 – All from Ian Logan Collection. 258/259 – Photo by Arthur Rothstein, Library of Congress. 270/271 – Chris Willemsen, 123rf.com.

Index

A Note on the Type

This book is typeset in Berthold Akzidenz-
Grotesk, a pioneering sans-serif font created
by the Berthold type foundry in Berlin in 1898.
A monoline font in which all strokes of the
letters are of the same thickness, its clarity
and simplicity contrasted strongly with the
ornate typefaces widely favoured in the late
19th century, and prefigured the clean lines of
20th-century fonts such as Helvetica. The firm's
founder, Hermann Berthold (1831–1904), was
also responsible for standardizing the system
of points used to measure type size.

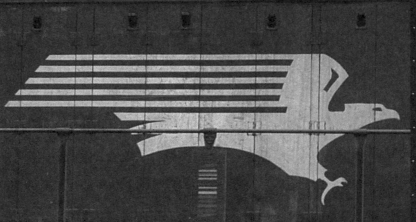